A Chair *with a* View

To Sava,
And to your
healing + growth

Best,
[signature] PhD.
8·27·18

Scenes of Heartbreak
and Breakthrough in Psychotherapy

DAVID M. SABINE, Ph.D.

Well Found
BOOKS

A Chair with a View
by David Sabine, PhD.

Copyright © 2012 Well Found Books

ISBN 978-0-9835740-0-2

FIRST EDITION
Library of Congress Cataloging-inPublication Data has been applied for.

Cover and interior design
by GKS Creative
gkscreative.com

Printed in the United States of America

DEDICATION

This book is dedicated to my four children:

Lauren, who taught me first through the bright blue eyes of a toddler and now in adulthood as a model of courage and integrity.

Ryan, the adventurer, whose essential exuberance and passion may be the best evidence I know of the goodness of life.

Abby, almost lost to us as a baby, but who returned with a tender heart and fierce loyalty and whose love for her family and her pets still echoes the purity that is the essence of innocence.

And Ben, the tender, generous child of my middle years, who continues to come alongside his aging father to remind him that the best is always yet to come.

I love you all and always.

ACKNOWLEDGEMENTS

THE DEBT OF GRATITUDE in my life always exceeds my resources to repay. The first huge thank you goes to the indomitable Antoinette Kuritz, who wore all of the hats of publicist, project manager, editor, counselor, and unfailing believer in me and in this work. Thanks also to Martha Smith for editorial help, Gwyn Kennedy Snider for cover and interior design and layout, and Douglas Love for his copy edit. Thanks to Dave Caroll, for my photograph on the cover flap. And to James Hoggard, former Texas poet laureate, supreme mentor and critic, for suggestions and ideas, and who cared enough about writing and about me to occasionally utter the most valuable words spoken in this process, "David, that just doesn't work." To Dan Millman, who encouraged me with both his literary chops and his amazing soul. Those who know him and have read his work know what I mean. Thanks to my mother, Minnie Lou, whose devotion to God and to me are eternal, and who taught me about the worlds that await me in the words written down in books. And to my father, Dick Sabine, whose selflessness on behalf of those he loves is inexhaustible, and who shared with me the privilege of a million holes of golf. To my brother, Bruce, who came to love reading late, but rekindled my love for words well chosen. To Kay, the mother of my children, and one of the finest people I have ever known, who continues to grow to this day in wisdom and has remained my cherished friend in spite of my considerable failures. To Gage and Kameron, who cheered me on as I chased about the country in pursuit of the unlikely dream that yielded this work. Over the years there have been a host of people—patients, parishioners and friends— who have believed in me, and given generously of themselves. My thanks to you all. And finally, to my "Bella," Kelly, who was my dedicated partner in this work from conception to completion. Though struggling sometimes to find herself worthy of her dreams, she nevertheless found the courage to champion mine.

TABLE OF CONTENTS

PROLOGUE

Loyal hearts can change the face of Sorrow,
*Softly encircle it with love's most gentle **unearthly radiance.***
—DIETRICH BONHOEFFER

ON THE COUCH in my office sits a ten-year-old boy whose father killed himself just a week ago. The child's eyes are downcast. His blank stare is unfocused. He is not really present here, but in another place altogether . . . and not a pleasant place at all. Nothing about his expression is animated, as if he is wearing a mask that is devoid of any hint of life or emotion.

I know that face. That is the face of sorrow. Having seen it countless times in my years as a psychotherapist, I am still unnerved by it. That mask appears impenetrable, as if defying the audacious notion that I can do anything about it; that I can erase or even mitigate it.

Long ago I gave up the notion that I was smart or wise enough to banish sorrow from the room. But I have a secret. I know how to restrain sorrow, to limit its power to destroy and control. My method is imperfect, even improbable, but it is powerful. I want to invite you to see this process at work and experience it for yourself. Come in. Sit down in my chair. There is a portal here in my office through which you can see beyond sorrow and pain to where life opens up, where you can see through to the other side of loss. That portal, that process, is called psychotherapy.

Psychotherapy has been the butt of a thousand jokes and the subject of scores of movies and television shows that make light of its bold claims. I have no axe

"We dance around in a ring and suppose / But the Secret sits in the middle and knows."

to grind here. I am familiar with the fact that all too often psychotherapy fails to deliver what it has promised. But those characterizations are not the last word on this work. Here, you have a chance to sit in my chair and see through that portal for yourself—past pain, past loss, past sorrow, all the way to joy.

As Robert Frost wrote, "We dance around in a ring and suppose / But the Secret sits in the middle and knows."

The Holy of Holies

The most sacred place in the life of ancient Israel was the Holy of Holies, that space was where God was located. Sure, the Israelites believed God was everywhere. But in that tiny, central room in the tabernacle, the glory of God was at its most intense.

Anyone who was unclean was not permitted to enter the Holy of Holies. In fact, only once a year did any mortal venture there. After days of preparation, supplication, and repentance, the High Priest would go into the Holy of Holies. Legend has it that his ankle was tethered with a rope so that if God struck him dead because of some moral failing or uncleanliness, his fellow worshippers would have a way to recover his body and not have to leave him there to rot. If the High Priest was not able to enter and survive, certainly no one else would be able to either.

The Ark of the Covenant was inside the Holy of Holies. The children of Israel believed that God was inside the Ark. They could count on God's presence because they had the Ark in which he lived. In a way, they possessed God.

This whole idea seems primitive to us today—God in a box. But I find the image of the Holy of Holies rich and personal. The Holy of Holies may be any place that we recognize as a place where the depth and beauty of life shines through. For many, it might be the sanctuary of a church or synagogue. For the obstetrician, it might be the delivery room. For the artist, the studio. For the mountaineer, the summit.

For the therapist, the Holy of Holies is the office. This is the place where people come and confess; where, for a few moments, they are honest about their lives and their feelings. It bears some similarities to the Catholic confessional. Only, this confession is without absolution. The process is about work and courage, not about being excused.

The office is also where I, the therapist, need to be purged of self-interest, to be a vessel of grace and mercy, of acceptance and affirmation.

The office is also where I, the therapist, am challenged to be authentic. I need to be purged of self-interest, to be a vessel of grace and mercy, of acceptance and affirmation. I have been invited into the heart of suffering, to be fully present with grief, pain and longing; to not shrink, but be hopeful; to believe that death and loss will not have the last word. Something new, wonderful, or joyful might just happen. In this room, where Life has so often been revealed, it is impossible for me to sit down in my chair with a client in front of me, and not steal a look around the room in expectation of a visitation. This is, after all, the Holy of Holies.

The Office

Sigmund Freud was a pioneer of so-called "talk therapy." Although many of his ideas are controversial, there is no doubt he has greatly influenced the way we talk about ourselves and our experiences. Whenever we talk about ego or repression or denial or projection, we are tipping our hat to the man with the big cigar.

As a graduate student, I watched a documentary about Freud's office. The "couch" in his office was actually an amorphous blob that looked almost like a giant bean-bag chair. Visually, the couch itself was not interesting to me, even though it was to become an icon of the 20th century. What I found fascinating were the things that surrounded that chair. Throughout the office, there were antiquities from all over the world and across time. Art forms of human figures, in all manner of poses, surrounded the patients as they divulged their lives, their dreams, and their pain. I thought it was a brilliant arrangement. The patient would bring personal struggles and sit down to ponder them amid all of those symbols of connectedness to life and human history.

When I set out to create my own office fifteen years ago, I wanted to design a space that bore my own stamp but would also be a place that felt safe and encouraged reflection, a place that was at once comforting and challenging.

One influence on my plan was the Roman Catholic mass. Although I was raised in a Protestant denomination, my seminary training made me aware of the Catholic tradition that worship is experienced in all five senses: sight, sound, touch, taste, and smell. In the Catholic embrace of the senses, visual stimulation is provided by the beautiful, soaring cathedral. The sounds of the music, chants, and the mass engage the ear. Touch comes from the kneeling rail and the host on the tongue. The worshippers taste the host and smell the incense. I love that idea—that worship is not just an intellectual activity, but that grace is experienced in every sense.

So, I try to present an experience in psychotherapy that welcomes all five senses. Let me take you inside my office. You can see for yourself.

My office is in a large home built at the turn of the last century. Three levels measuring seventy-six hundred square feet, six fireplaces, and a hundred years of stories are enhanced by extraordinary craftsmanship, twelve-foot ceilings, and massive crown molding. As you climb the curving staircase, a simple, handmade rail rises with you in a graceful arc leading to the second story landing. Once you arrive at that landing, there is a simple door that opens into my office. Inside, a fireplace with a heavy wooden mantle is on the left. Windows flank the right and far wall, with floated glass panes that reflect and bend whatever you see outside in an other-worldly way.

Two themes guide the decoration–sailing and books. I am a sailor, and when I travel, I like to charter a sailboat and island-hop for a few days. Sailing is an apt metaphor for life, I think, and there are many nautical artifacts around the office. Model sailing vessels, a ship's wheel, an antique copper deep-sea diver's helmet, and a miniature lighthouse can be found about the room. Pictures of sailboats and nautical maps decorate the walls. Sailing is simple and elegant, and it implies the potential for fear and adventure, for peace and peril—like life.

Books are everywhere—on the credenzas, on the mantle, and filling a large bookcase. There are not many books about psychology or therapy. Poetry, literature, and philosophy dominate. The works of Shakespeare fill one shelf.

On the far wall is a couch, and just to the right of it is a leather chair. As you sit down, notice how soft and forgiving that chair is. A candle gives off a subtle and pleasant incense. The fragrance lasts just long enough to say 'welcome' and then has the good manners to slip unobtrusively into the background. You will find your choice of coffee, tea, or soft drink to ensure your sense of taste is also included.

The holy sounds of pain and loss will be heard here soon. But those sounds will be cradled in this sensory refuge, which echoes and reverberates with acceptance and affirmation.

I want to share with you my experience of sitting here with patients while they tell me their stories. I will disclose what they say and what their words do to me. You will see how this arrangement changes us both.

Thomas Szasz, the iconoclastic critic of "mental health treatment," states, "There is no psychology; there is only biography and autobiography." I agree. The stories that

> "There is no psychology; there is only biography and autobiography."

follow are biography and autobiography. As I share the stories of ten remarkable people, I am sharing my own story at the same time. The experience of each of these people has affected my story. This improvisational dance of stories is called psychotherapy.

The variety of problems brought to this sanctuary is staggering: *My mother was abusive. My husband is cheating. I am cheating. I lost my dog. I have cancer. I have AIDS. No one loves me. I am afraid to quit my job. I can't stop pulling out my hair. I have thoughts that are so bad I can't tell anyone about them. I just want to die.* The list goes on and on. None of these concerns are trivial, but each points to a need for meaning.

In one form or another, the question is "what does life mean if this is so?" While I never know what the exact meaning is in a particular problem, I am confident that the patient and I can find a way to create meaning out of it. Some issues are easier than others. I can more easily help a client find the meaning in a lost job than in a lost son or daughter. In simple terms, this is the gift of being human.

While I never know what the exact meaning is in a particular problem, I am confident that the patient and I can find a way to create meaning out of it.

We are the only species capable of conceptualizing something as abstract as "meaning." It amazes me that we can create it as well.

The work is often laborious, sometimes tedious, but once in a while transcendent, luminous, and deep. Here, patients discover, assign and experience meaning in their existences. Sometimes, we therapists find meaning for ourselves in the process. Not a bad way to spend my days.

Psychotherapy and Time

What if we were not confined by the ineffable, relentless march of time? I have watched the supple, translucent skin of my youth degrade until I now seem to be enveloped in my father's skin instead. It bears the marks of abuse by sun and wind. My once uniform complexion now yields to a random patchwork of color and texture, pre-figuring the loose epidermal drape that will one day encase my corpse. Cosmetics companies have made billions on the tantalizing promise that they have captured youth in a bottle. Their carefully researched formulas, they claim, will set Old Man Time on his heels and restore what he had taken away. Wouldn't that be nice?

Time robs us of far more than physical vitality. One by one, he also steals those with whom we share this amazing life. Sometimes gradually, sometimes with swift and brutal precision, time wrests us from our parents, our life-long partners, and all too often, even the ones furthest from old age, our children. Inevitably, time will come for each of us and send us on to the next stop, without even the good form to tell us where we are going and what is next.

Though we mark days in hours and minutes, we are mystified by the way time sometimes bends. When we are bored, time drags. When we are having fun, "time flies." When we are thwarted, we lose time. When we hurry, we can make up time.

But for me, time has some special meanings. To frame these meanings, I will appeal to a concept from an ancient form of Greek.

In Koine Greek, there are two words for time. *Chronos* is the linear time we experience in everyday life. There is a sense of then, and now, and later. This is the "terrifying plane" of life. On this plane we see the horizon of birth and death. The singular realization that we are transitory and ephemeral, here for a moment and then gone, troubles all of us.

> *The singular realization that we are transitory and ephemeral, here for a moment and then gone, troubles all of us.*

The other idea of time in Greek is *Kairos*. This notion is unfamiliar to us and is more difficult to understand. This form of time transcends *Chronos*. It is an experience where all of *Chronos* is caught up together. The philosophers sometimes refer to this concept as "the Eternal Now."

I remember one of my many moments of *Kairos*. I was married and living in Fort Worth's inner city. Our first-born, Lauren, had just turned three. It was a summer Saturday evening, and I had just given her a bath. She was perfect— fine blond hair, riveting blue eyes. Smelling that wonderful baby shampoo and powder fragrance known to all parents, I carried her out to the porch, pulling a chair along. Sitting down, I settled her into my arms with her head on my chest. I watched as the day wound down. Children ran or rode their bikes up and down the street. The heat of the summer day had broken and a light breeze blew through the porch.

As I took in my world, I slipped into a moment of *Kairos*. At that instant, from where we sat together, I captured the whole stretch of *Chronos*. My mind's eye saw the day she was born. I saw her mother and me getting married. I saw the day my parents married. I saw the day Lauren would get married. Time continued to expand. When the image of the day I will die came to my mind, I was not troubled at all, partly because that thought sat right next to the moment when I was born. In fact, from this perspective, both moments seemed to happen "now." From this vantage, the overwhelming feeling was joy. Grief, loss, all the longings of life existed only on the plane of *Chronos*. *Kairos* was a triumphant time perspective. Interestingly, this didn't seem to be the moment when the theology of my youth was confirmed—that God was standing somewhere above *Kairos*. Instead, the

Divine seemed evident *everywhere in Kairos*, as part of its mystery.

Since then, these moments of *Kairos* have happened to me many times. I have experienced it as each of my four children made the difficult and mysterious passage into life. Other moments of *Kairos* have come at joyous celebrations of marriage and in quiet moments of worship. I also feel *Kairos* in moments of physical intimacy, when sex and passion open the door to the depth and richness of life.

Perhaps my most arresting moments of Kairos have arrived in times of great sorrow. As a minister in my early adulthood, I conducted many funerals, and I came to almost feel guilty about how I experienced those solemn rituals. The congregation was in unbearable pain, but I could not help looking around the sanctuary thinking, "I know it is here." I didn't know if that moment would be ushered in by a song, or the eulogy, or perhaps the countenance of a particular mourner. But inevitably, the moment would break through, and I would feel the deep resonance of *Kairos* beginning to reverberate inside me as *Chronos* gave way. Tears would come, but not tears of sorrow. Perhaps they were tears that simply acknowledged the presence of *Kairos*. Perhaps those tears overflowed because the abundance of that moment could not be contained.

> *It is not until you recognize that the whole is nothing but more of the same perfect essence, that you realize the scope of life's underlying goodness.*

As I have cobbled together these moments of *Kairos*, what seemed at first like random blessings have become a pattern. Life is a honeycomb: From the outside, life sometimes appears random, amorphous, and gray. Then, when a drop of honey hits your tongue, it seems a miracle that something so wonderful comes from such an unlikely place. What is inside the honeycomb is not random at all. It is an intricate series of discreet cells, each of which offers a passage to that amazing sweetness that is the essence of the whole thing. One moment of *Kairos* is like one cell of the honeycomb. It has everything in it that every other cell has. But it is not until you recognize that the whole is nothing but more of the same perfect essence, that you realize the scope of life's underlying goodness.

I believe that the healing work of psychotherapy provides moments of *Kairos* right here in this room. Client after client has described to me a moment in a particular session of being transported to another perspective, from which life was seen differently, and the sorrows that led to seeking treatment were transcended. Nothing had changed in my client's outward circumstance, but nothing was the same afterwards. Once this breakthrough came, I knew the better part of the work was done. Clients might come back for a while, but more for consolidation and celebration than anything else. They would soon take that transcendent experience out into the *Chronos* of their own lives. No, they had not been perfected. They still harbored problems, pain and suffering. But from this point forward, the pain of *Chronos,* with all its sad vagaries of loss and death, would hopefully not have the power to mire and terrorize them. They could experience life with greater courage and deeper joy because of this great gift.

To clarify, this is not a gift that I *give* my clients. I don't know how to *make* this happen for anyone. I simply try to be faithful to my task, with patience and readiness, believing that the two of us can get there together.

I hope my orientation into the mysterious work of psychotherapy helps you absorb the stories that follow. Each story was selected carefully. First, I chose stories that reveal the experience of pain, the dubious inheritance of all people. But pain is met in these particular journeys in an especially beautiful or heroic way. Next, I selected stories that, for whatever reason, moved or challenged or changed me. Finally, I selected stories that reveal how the relationship between therapist and patient works to support real change.

An additional chapter is about my friend Daryl, the one story in the book that is not about a patient. I have included it because my relationship with Daryl had a great deal to do with my becoming a psychologist.

All of the other stories are about real patients. They are true stories, with the exception of details that have been changed to protect confidentiality. One story represents a blending of two lives that were remarkably parallel. Except for the stories of Lillie and Betty, all of the patients' names are changed.

Lillie is deceased. Her grandson, and executor of her estate, read and approved the manuscript. He was also kind enough to supply me with Lillie's journal, which was instrumental in the telling of her story. Why her name was left unchanged will become apparent as you follow her tale.

When Betty read my chapter about her, she gave me permission to use the story with the condition that I use her real name. She felt that the telling of her story, and the claiming of that story as her own, was vitally important to her, again for reasons that will become evident.

All of the major characters have read and approved their stories. We discussed the possible downsides and benefits to them personally, and they generously agreed to take part, each expressing the hope that his or her story would be an encouragement to all who read it.

My own goal in rendering these journeys, however, is not simply my need to share them. They are a product of my own desire to extend a glimpse into the beauty of life, as I so often see it in my therapy office. For the last fifteen years, this work has been my personal calling. Hopefully, without the taint of preachment or personal arrogance, I will engage in a sort of relationship with you, too, as we explore this mystery together.

In the Christian tradition of Communion, sometimes called the Lord's Supper, the members of the community of faith sit side by side as they bear witness to the shared experience of the great beauty and depth of Life, symbolically represented by the bread and wine. The worshippers are sometimes called "communicants," literally, "those to whom something is imparted." Over these next pages, come sit with me as a fellow communicant. Enter into the experience of these remarkable souls, and, together, we will witness both heartbreak and breakthrough, the major chords of this work. As the old proverb says, "They that sow in tears will reap in joy."

So, prepare yourself. If you are ready, rest yourself in my chair. Get comfortable. And let me introduce you to Rose.

chapter one

THE BOX

And then the risk it took
To remain tight in a bud
Was more painful than
The risk it took to blossom.

       - *ANAIS NIN*

IN MY OFFICE, there is a box that has sat undisturbed for the past five years. Not a box from a store, but an ornate, handcrafted one about the size of a large box of wooden matches. The sides are maroon velvet, and the top is inlaid with mother of pearl. It bears the look of a treasure box, where something precious or sacred is stored. It is full of small objects, each identical to the others, but each is remarkable for what it represents. The box is full of razor blades.

Each blade stands for a moment when, for one particular girl, the invitation to pain was a siren's song, beckoning, promising her a sweet moment of release from her deadened interior. She had carefully constructed a life of mirrors reflecting what she thought the world wanted to see; but she had hidden another world, existing on a darker, more desperate plane.

During our first meeting, Rose seemed a hidden child. Although she was sitting in front of me, hair hanging in her face, cross-legged on my couch and wearing baggy jeans, I had the feeling that I wasn't seeing much of her at all. Without looking up, she waited, shrinking into the sofa, into herself, as if whatever would come next would certainly be an assault on her jealously guarded privacy.

"Rose, what brings us together?"

Slowly, the shoulders of her oversized sweatshirt lifted in a shrug. She shifted back and forth once, and she struggled to lift her gaze before her eyes fell back to the spot on the floor that had captivated her concentration since her arrival.

Waiting even a few seconds longer for her to answer seemed cruel. I wanted to fill the space, to assure her she was safe here and that she could talk to me. But I could see that feeling safe was a luxury she would not allow herself.

Finally, I relented and broke the silence. "Rose, would you like a glass of water?"

From behind the strands of hair came her first words, soft and thin and wavering. "Yes, please."

I got up out of my chair, walked to the desk a few feet away, and filled two glasses from a clear pitcher. I offered one to Rose. She looked at the glass and my extended hand. Slowly, she reached out and took it from me. By that simple gesture of accepting the water, she courageously allowed me to approach. This was our first step toward one another.

Rose was sixteen years old, one of two children born to a sullen, withholding father and a disabled, addicted mother. Her father was a long-term, low-level manager for a retail chain. Rose feared her father. He had a beef with life for denying him his dreams, leaving him in a dead-end job, and deserting him in a crappy North Texas town not far from the end of the earth, as far as he was concerned. Rose believed her father saw her as emblematic of his sorrow and looked at her with contempt. As far as she could remember, he had never stroked her hair as a girl, never looked on her with a smile, never said, "That's great, honey," "I love you," or any other of a thousand things that might have given her a reason to believe she mattered to him. That neglect, which swept through her childhood, seemed benign compared to the toxic sarcasm he rained down on her once she reached adolescence. Even though she said she wouldn't even know how to hope for a boyfriend, he called her "slut" and "whore," and constantly accused her of "wanting to sleep with every swinging dick that comes along." He was most cruel when he criticized her looks. Every blemish on her face, every added pound, every blush or tear, amused him, reinforcing her opinion that she was a loser.

Her mother was disabled with chronic back pain and had a tenacious addiction to Percocet. She spent most of the days in bed, calling Rose to compel her to make her dinner, bring her a pill, or clean the house. Rather than protect her daughter from her husband's maltreatment, her mother seemed immune, or perhaps amused, when his wrath came down.

Rose's brother was handsome, resilient, and a master of whatever he wished to do. He rose above his father's anger and his mother's misery without effort. According to Rose, she was weak and cowardly in his eyes for not doing the same. Over time, she came to despise his condescension. She was jealous of his ability to break free of their family's self-destructive gravity.

School had once been a sanctuary where her love of reading had fostered good grades. Now it was a place of particular torment, this time at the hands of her peers. The more they teased her, the more she shrank, fueling the bullying. Finally, Rose had retreated to the point where she disappeared inside herself. She wore big, nondescript clothing that hid her figure. Believing the belittling comments of her detractors, she grew out her bangs to keep the world from seeing her ugliness.

When Rose heard about me from one of my former clients and came to see me for the first time, she wore her pain like sackcloth and ashes. Anyone could see this girl was in trouble. Still, not all of Rose's pain was visible. Her biggest secret was at once her most private pleasure and her deepest shame.

I wondered if Rose would return after that first session. Could she bear to come again knowing that the very nature of our meeting was to look inside her experience as a team? Likely, that must have been a frightening idea to her. But she did return, revealing courage, character, and great need.

In the second session, Rose appeared as tentative as she had in the first.

"I'm not sure why I am coming here. I have no idea what I am doing."

"Rose," I said. "You don't have to figure all of that out just yet. We are just getting to know one another. Last week you did a great job sharing your story with me. But that was just the beginning."

"Well, how is this supposed to work?" she asked.

"You might be surprised to hear I have no idea."

Rose managed a weak smile. "Well, if you don't know, we are in big trouble."

"I know that sounds a little crazy, but I actually mean it," I replied. "I have worked with many people, but I have never worked with *you* before. So you and I will figure out what we need to do."

"I wouldn't know the first thing about how to figure that out."

"That's the beauty of this thing we are doing. Neither one of us knows just yet what our work will look like, but if you can hang with me a little while, I know it will come to us. It always seems to happen."

"But you have no idea how screwed up I am. I'm just going to waste your time," she said.

"Rose, this is your time and I am glad you are here. We are all screwed up in some way or another. I wouldn't know how to relate to someone who wasn't screwed up."

Rose shifted on the couch, another wan smile on her face.

"You are a unique person," I said. "We'll have to construct a plan just for you."

"I'm never sure there's hope for me."

I wanted to jump in and reassure her. There was something I really liked about Rose, although I couldn't put my finger on it. She definitely made me inclined to try to save her. After hearing the previous week about the abusive treatment by her family and the merciless teasing by her peers, I wanted to take her in and rescue her from everything she endured. Fortunately, I knew better. Somewhere, Rose had the strength to make her way out of this pain. Neither I nor anyone else would serve her well by indulging rescue fantasies. That would only rob her of discovering her own gifts, however deeply buried they were at the time.

I sat, waited, and finally reflected, "You feel hopeless."

"Yes. All the time. You think you know how messed up I am, but you don't."

I chose not to explore that provocative statement just yet.

Through the remainder of the session, Rose and I revisited the themes of the first session: rejection, inadequacy, and the cruelty of others. I continued to grapple with feelings of protectiveness. I wanted to corner those kids at school and give her parents a piece of my mind. I was pulled toward colluding with Rose in her despair.

In the next two sessions, Rose revealed more of her pain. She was stuck in a cycle of self-pity and hopelessness, fueled by the abuse from others and her own belief that at some level, she deserved the treatment she got. How was she going to pull herself out of this vicious spiral? I already cared deeply for Rose, but I had no idea just what shape the work we needed to do should look like. Each session, she seemed to take another step closer to fully revealing herself to me. Even though I was encouraged by her growing self-revelation, something was still unspoken.

In our fifth session, Rose took a remarkable step toward trusting me.

"Doc, I just don't know how to move ahead. My father hates me. My mother couldn't care less about me. My brother, supposedly the healthy one, despises me. Other girls hate me, too. And hell, the boys just love to make fun of me. After a while, I had to admit that they were right. I really am a screw-up, more than any of them will ever know."

"Rose, after hearing your story, I see it differently. I am impressed with how you continue, even though every aspect of your life seems to be painful. You are still here. Maybe you are stronger than you think. You have survived some of the toughest things life brings."

Rose sat very still for a few seconds, then said, "It's worse than you think, Doc. You want to know how I do it?"

I didn't say anything. I sensed that she was gathering herself to let me in, and I feared that open encouragement might feel like pressure and send her back behind the wall. Instead, I just waited.

My office sometimes feels like a sanctuary, a place where gargoyles chase away the demons and the angels lean in. At that moment, the office felt like a holy place, where the beauty of life was approaching, not so much to be seen by us, but to see us, to recognize us, and to invite us to draw close. The silence was heart-stopping.

Rose drew one deep breath and placed her right hand on her left wrist, and pulled the sleeve of her old sweatshirt up past her elbow. With her head down, she turned her arm over to reveal the inside of her wrist and forearm.

The visible record of her pain started just above the heel of her hand and continued the length of her forearm. Hundreds of scars, neatly and deliberately aligned, some old, some new, registered her anger, loneliness, and despair.

"My legs are a lot worse," she confessed.

As I looked at Rose's arm, I realized that something was happening that I had not expected. Suddenly, I became aware that Rose had raised her head and was looking at me. Now, I wondered what she expected to see on my face, an expression of horror or revulsion perhaps? At that moment, something guided me to raise my eyes to meet hers. Instead of morbidly lingering on her shame or looking away in disgust, I looked up into her eyes and met her gaze. To my great surprise, she did not look away. Face to face, eyes locked, we really met for the very first time.

Without looking away, I heard myself say, "Thank you so much, Rose."

A tear that formed in her unblinking eyes slid down her cheek to her trembling chin. She seemed to understand that my thank you was more than a recognition of her courage in showing me the tangible, scarred record of her grief. It also acknowledged that she had permitted me into her interior world, part inner sanctum and part chamber of horrors, and she had trusted that I would not shrink or retreat. As my own eyes welled up, my gratitude overcame me.

Scores of patients have come to me through the years as a result of the seductive call to cut and carve upon their own skin. The reasons for the self-mutilations are complex. Some say it is to let out the pain they feel inside. Others report they already feel numb or dead, and that the pain that comes from cutting reminds them they are still alive. Some do it in a kind of romantic dance with teenage angst. They chat online with other people about their pain and then find solace and companionship in the shared ritual of blood-letting.

Some say it hurts. Others say it doesn't. Incredibly, some compare it to the ecstasy of orgasm, a powerful and pleasurable release.

But I had never seen anyone who had carried it so far as Rose. Most cutting is discovered early and does not happen frequently. But Rose didn't have anyone who seemed to be paying attention. No one noticed that she never wore sleeveless shirts or shorts, or let anyone see her arms or legs. She had not confided to anyone, on-line or elsewhere. Hers was a solitary ceremony, carried out hundreds of times with no witnesses but her own sorrow.

"Doc, I cut when I'm lonely. I cut when my Dad yells at me. I cut when I am reminded that no boy would ever want a freak like me. Hell, these days I cut just because I am bored."

"Have you ever tried to stop?" I asked.

"For a while, every time I cut, I would feel such shame that I would make a solemn promise never to do it again. And then I would. Over and over. And each time I did it, the shame got worse. Finally, I just stopped kidding myself. I can't stop. I don't think I ever will. I honestly don't want to. It's all I have."

Rose was stuck. She had been sad for so long. The rejection and humiliation she had endured was no longer just in her father's derision, her brother's condescension, or her peers' brutality. Tragically, Rose's desperate attempt to slam the door on those who seemed to delight in torturing her came too late. The demons of rejection and humiliation had already slipped inside. The torturers were now internalized and more powerful than ever, wreaking havoc in the narrow corridors of her broken heart. In the confines of her self-imposed exile, cutting was the only way to remind herself what it felt like to be alive. Once she was numbed from all other emotions, only the primitive experience of physical pain remained.

When she slammed the door on her tormentors, she isolated herself from good things as well.

Unfortunately, when she slammed the door on her tormentors, she isolated herself from good things as well. Feeling a hug through a closed and locked door is hard to accomplish. You can never know the comfort that comes from the warm and tender touch of another person when you dare not open the door to welcome them in.

In spite of my powerful wish to reach out to Rose, I had to resign myself to standing outside and knocking. Her door opened only from the inside. Her pain kept her coming to sessions, but despite fleeting moments of connection we still seemed to be regarding each other from a distance.

As we approached the sixth session, I knew I needed a way to bridge the chasm between us. Necessity being the mother of invention, I thought I might try something different. I suggested to Rose that we watch a movie together during our sessions.

You can never know the comfort that comes from the warm and tender touch of another person when you dare not open the door to welcome them in.

Yes, I know that insurance policies probably don't cover "cinema therapy" in their "evidence- based protocols," but the idea made some sense to me.

Hollywood is the mecca of American culture. It is the sanctuary where we pay tribute to the power of story to teach us about ourselves and each other. There in the dark, titillated by flickering visions, we are able to grieve our intransigent mortality, we feel our hearts quicken as we embrace the infatuations of love that may have otherwise faded in memory, and we exult in the triumph of the heroic over evil, which is the ultimate victory to which we aspire.

For me, the movies are more than a passion. They are an obsession born of deprivation. I was raised in a conservative, evangelical denomination called the Church of the Nazarene. We aspired to be especially "holy" people, committed to avoiding the "appearance of evil." The wearing of shorts and tank-tops was frowned upon. I never went to a high school dance (Such behavior encourages fornication!). We were not allowed to go to a swimming pool where people of the opposite sex might be present in their swimwear. Our Manual called this prohibited conduct "mixed bathing." The Manual was the official book of rules produced by the Church, apparently because the Bible was not clear enough about how to conduct oneself.

More than any other prohibition, I hated the rule prohibiting the Hollywood motion picture. Growing up, I was never allowed to go to the movies. I never saw *Doctor Zhivago, Butch Cassidy and the Sundance Kid,* or *Jaws.* I never even delighted in a Disney film. Musicals like *The Sound of Music, My Fair Lady,* or *The Wizard of Oz* had to wait until they were carved up into pieces on broadcast TV to allow for commercials. I never saw the inside of a theater or a "big screen." It is hard to estimate how this deprivation affected my generation of young "Nazarenes." For our contemporaries, the movies were one of the primary sources of community.

After graduating from the Nazarene seminary, I teamed up with an amazing fellow student named Bryan Stone. Bryan and I founded a ministry called "Liberation Community" in an inner city neighborhood in Fort Worth, Texas. From time to time, Bryan and I would hit the road to raise money for the ministry by speaking at various churches in the area.

One night, Bryan and I were enjoying a meal at a Denny's restaurant in

Amarillo after we had spoken in the Sunday Night service at one of the local Churches of the Nazarene. Bryan was a clever guy, brilliant in fact, and I was always trying to play catch up to his wit and mental agility.

That night, he posed a hypothetical question: "David, let's say you went back to your hotel room tonight and a criminal had broken in and held you at gunpoint. He tells you the bad news that he is about to kill you. But first, he will allow you to write anything you want in twenty-five words or less on a piece of paper. What would you write?"

I pondered this carefully. I knew Bryan to be a serious thinker and he must have his own idea that would certainly be quite impressive. The best I could come up with was *"Find the man who killed and forgive him."* Wow. Not bad, huh? A radical Christian response if there ever was one.

Bryan smiled and agreed. "Not bad."

I enjoyed his approval, but I knew there was lightning coming in his response.

"Well, what would you say?" I asked.

Grinning, Bryan opened a napkin, jotted down his response, and held it out for me to read.

I was prepared for a thoughtful theological treatise in twenty-five words or less. Instead, I opened it and read his simple statement: *"The Church of the Nazarene is wrong about the movies."*

You would have to come from that tidy enclave in which we were raised to appreciate how funny that moment was and to understand how deeply we resented the church's untenable stance about the movies. As usual, Bryan had captured a truth perfectly. This seemingly trivial issue between two young men and the church in which they had trained to serve was actually a big deal.

Not only did we disagree with the stance the church had taken, but we sensed something magical and graceful about the movies and their powerful ability to communicate. Yes, the movies can sometimes communicate messages of exploitation and dehumanization. But they also reach us with truth, beauty, and passion. Maybe you can imagine how I felt when I finally broke with my upbringing at eighteen-years-old and snuck into line to see *Star Wars!*

Ironically, Bryan went on to be a professor in the Religion Department of Boston University, where he soon wrote a wonderful book titled *Faith and Film.*

In the book, he explores and illustrates the Apostle's Creed in a dozen or so Hollywood films. Bryan and I don't see each other much these days, but when we do, we talk about movies we have discovered of late. We both seem to have overcome that childhood taboo.

That brings me back to Jesus and the movies, although the two are now on the same side. The ministry of Jesus, as recounted in the Bible, suggests to me that if Jesus were walking the earth today, he might well appear as a filmmaker. Jesus seemed inclined to tap the power of story through parables: "The Prodigal Son," "The Unjust Judge," and "The Widow's Mite" were the movies of his day.

Perhaps Jesus sensed that people were resistant to new ideas that challenged their safe assumptions about life and the world. Maybe we still are too ensconced in the *status quo* of our lives to hear the truth about ourselves directly. Jesus would tell a story to willing listeners. I have often thought that people in attendance might have left one of Jesus's teachings saying, "I loved that story he told about the Pearl of Great Price!" Then later, as they recalled the story, they would understand the personal connection. "That story was about me and my life!"

> *Even though our conscious mind stands guard, story has the power to slip under our defenses and insinuate itself into our hearts, until suddenly we realize who we really are or what we must do.*

Indeed, even though our conscious mind stands guard, story has the power to slip under our defenses and insinuate itself into our hearts, until suddenly we realize who we really are or what we must do.

Given my history, the idea of using a movie as a tool in Rose's psychotherapy was no surprise—a little unorthodox, perhaps, but not unlikely. The movie I thought was fitting was *My First Mister*, a seldom seen but well-reviewed film starring Albert Brooks as Randall, a stuffy, obsessive-compulsive mall store manager, and Leelee Sobieski as an angst-ridden teenager called J.

J, dressed in Gothic-style clothing with piercings over her face and ears, sits alone and cuts herself. She writes poems with themes of pain and suicide, which she then folds into paper airplanes to fly from her bedroom window. Her mother is annoying. Her stepfather ignores her. Her pot-smoking, hippy father is oblivious. She is adrift and angry.

J begins to look for a job and is hired by Randall on the condition that "you take all that metal out of your face." At first, the tension between the two has a sharp edge, not unlike her razor blades. They draw metaphorical blood from each other, never slicing an actual vein but certainly inflicting pain.

Over time, they form an unlikely friendship. With Randall's bumbling help, J manages to find peace with herself and acceptance of her life. The film is a charming, warm, and moving story about the power of relationship and how it unexpectedly compels us into knowledge of our purpose here and courage to embrace the life that just yesterday may have seemed not worth living.

The power of relationship unexpectedly compels us into knowledge of our purpose here and courage to embrace the life that just yesterday may have seemed not worth living.

Like the character J, Rose was alienated from herself and the world. I wanted her to see the same beauty and strength I could envision in her, but I knew she would never be able to hear it directly from me. Maybe the film would do what I could not. Perhaps the positive power of the relationship between J and Randall would help Rose feel hopeful and recognize that our relationship might become a vehicle to take her to new, promising places.

Instead of the face-to-face encounters that typically characterized our weekly sessions, watching the film situated us side-by-side, sharing the experience together. Because our sessions only lasted forty-five minutes, we had to break the viewing into several sessions. Rose watched quietly but attentively. Even though I had seen the film several times before, watching it with Rose was powerful and affecting for me. I sensed that she was identifying with J's pain, and I was able to identify with Rose's pain more immediately as well.

When *My First Mister* was over, I resisted the temptation to review the parallels and lessons that I think the film offers, trusting instead Rose's ability to take from it what she needed. The film's power would only be diluted by my trying to spell it out.

After the movie, Rose seemed more able to talk directly about her cutting. We returned to the topic more and more as the weeks passed. We headed out on new issues as well, but this one behavior remained the centerpiece. It had come to define her. Although it offered only a momentary release from pain, it extinguished the hope that the future would offer anything she might want or need.

One day, the procedural steps in her cutting were the focus of our talk.

"Well, I always do it in my room. I lock the door and get the box out from under the bed."

"The box?" I queried.

"Yeah. I have a box I made," she said. "I put all my blades in there. I made it myself. It took a long time, but I think it is beautiful. It's the most precious thing that I have."

"I would love to see it," I said.

"You would? Why?"

"Well," I replied, "because it is very important to you, I wondered if you would show it to me, if you want to."

"I'll think about it," she stated simply. With that, we moved on.

Rose came to the session the next week carrying something small wrapped in a plastic bag. She sat it down next to her on the couch and looked up, ostensibly waiting for me to begin the session. I looked at her, then down to the bag, and then back to her.

Rose squirmed in her seat, obviously anxious.

"I brought the box to show you," she announced.

"Are you sure you want to? You don't have to just because I asked."

"Don't you want to see it?" she replied.

I realized I had worked us into a little bind. I had asked her to bring the box, and now I was asking her if she really wanted to show it to me. That might confuse anyone.

"Rose, I would love to see it," I assured her. "You had the courage to bring it. If you want to go ahead, we can talk about it."

With that, she took a deep breath and moved the package to her lap, gently holding it in her hands. She looked up at me for a moment and then back down, still very hesitant.

"No one else has seen this before. I have hidden it for two years."

Rose unfolded the bag, reached inside, and pulled out the box. Moving the bag aside, she held it with both hands before extending it toward me. She clearly was not just showing it. She wanted me to hold it.

She looked at me as I took it, but her eyes immediately dropped back to the box. I watched her face staring at her most precious belonging, now in someone else's hands.

"It's very beautiful, Rose," I said appreciatively. I remained still, awaiting her instruction.

"Open it ... if you want to," she said quietly.

I slowly lifted the lid and peered inside. There were dozens of razor blades haphazardly thrown in one by one. Rather than the single-edged razor blades one might typically imagine, these were all small blades that fit into Exacto knives. They all looked unused and showed no sign of blood. Each of them had been meticulously cleaned before it had been deposited here.

"I used each of them one time, then I threw them in there," she said. "I have been saving every one of them from the beginning."

"Why save them?" I asked.

"Those blades represent the story of my life—all the pain, all the hurt. It's all contained in that box."

"Actually," she continued, "I don't know what I have except for those memories. It's by thinking about them that I know I'm still alive."

"How long do you think you'll keep this box?" I asked.

"That's a good question, Doc. I was wondering if you might keep it for me for a while."

I have never been so humbled by a charge a patient has given me. She was entrusting with me her most personal, treasured possession. I was truly moved—and hopeful.

"I promise I won't cut while you're keeping the box for me," Rose said. "If I need it, will you give it back to me?"

The question troubled me. I was moved that she wanted to stop cutting, but I foresaw a dilemma. What if she came back in a week, or a month, and wanted the box back? Would I be able to give it back in good conscience? In spite of that possibility, I couldn't decline her offer.

The sailor who ventures out of the safe confines of the lake or river to take to the open ocean often refers to a phenomenon called a "sea change." This refers to a change in the way the waves and current are behaving. Sometimes the change is obvious and the sailor knows immediately how to shift the set of the sails. At other times, the change is subtle, more difficult to detect, but something is still different. When a sea change happens, the craft is borne along by a new set of circumstances, by forces exerting a different series of contingencies, and calling for a new response.

In the act of surrendering her box of razor blades, Rose relinquished her secret shame. But she didn't throw it away, or destroy it. Perhaps that would have meant something else if she had. But she gave it to a custodian to care for it in case she needed it again. One might suppose that by doing so she was equivocating, lacking a firm commitment. I wondered that myself.

As time passed, however, two things became evident—one obvious and one almost imperceptible. What was obvious was the trust Rose had placed in me. She not only charged me to take care of this precious artifact of her sorrow and pain, but she was also saying that I understood the significance of both the box and of her giving it to me.

What was far more subtle, beyond my ability to detect it at the time, was that Rose's presentation signaled a sea change. With that one act of courage, she was proclaiming her value as a person, a person who did not deserve to be repeatedly injured either by others or by her own hand. She was setting her course away from the rage and shame and heartbreak that had once compelled her. She was steering toward a new bearing. That new direction would not be without its challenges. Storms would still rise up and there would be days when the wind refused to blow. But Rose had come to believe that this new destination was perhaps just over the horizon. And she knew now that she would find her way to that sheltered cove, and the safety for which she had longed.

With that one act of courage, she was proclaiming her value as a person, a person who did not deserve to be repeatedly injured either by others or by her own hand.

That was five years ago, and Rose has never asked me to return her box. After that transcendent moment of surrender, Rose came back for a few sessions, and we worked on the basic tools of communication and assertiveness that she would need on her adventure. Before long, Rose had shown such progress that we arranged a termination session.

The day Rose saw me for the last time felt like a graduation day, and I suppose it was. It was a commencement in the best sense of the word. Rose was moving on. She was launching beyond the safety of our relationship and giving it a go all on her own. And I could not have been more proud.

After we had rehearsed the substance of our work together, the time came for the session to end. I found, mixed in with all of my pride and excitement for Rose, a personal sadness that we had come to an end in our relationship. I was going to miss her.

As I opened the door for Rose to leave my office and my life, she paused and smiled tenderly and said very simply, "Thanks Doc."

I smiled back, "You are welcome, Rose. Go have the life you deserve. I am pulling for you."

"I know you are," she said, and then she looked away from me at what lay ahead of her, first the stairs leading down from my office and then out into her life.

One of the most difficult things about being a psychotherapist is that patients move on with their lives and rarely give me a follow-up or update, so I don't know if the depression went away, if the marriage survived, if the panic attacks resolved, or the voices returned. I am committed to and involved with them for an intense piece of their lives. Then, despite the best professional intention, they move into their futures without me. That is as it should be. But once in a while, I get a hint that restores my hope.

Almost exactly one year after Rose had left therapy, I received a beautiful invitation in the mail—a wedding invitation—to Rose's wedding. I didn't feel it was appropriate to actually attend the wedding. After all, how would I explain my presence sitting on the bride's side with tears in my eyes and a silly grin on my face? How would I explain to anyone that I know the triumphant significance of this day, that the beautiful woman who is standing in front of everyone present is claiming her right to be loved and honored?

No, I couldn't go. But I get it, Rose. I really get it.

chapter two

LILLIE BELLE

Can I see another's woe, and
not be in sorrow too?
Can I see another's grief, and
not seek for kind relief?
—*WILLIAM BLAKE*

LILLIE IS ELDERLY, with beautiful white
hair and a smile that features one prominent
front tooth. Seated across from me in a wheelchair, she appears fragile. Her eyes
are faded with age but still retain the ability to flash dark with anger or to strike
up a sparkle when she laughs. Her appearance does not reveal that Lillie cannot
speak as you and I do. An occasional word or phrase is all she can manage.

When I was consulted one day in 1995 by the doctors at Wichita Falls
Rehabilitation Hospital to evaluate and treat a woman named Lillie Blacklock in
room 121, bed B, I had no idea what was in store for me—indeed for the two of us.

When a psychologist first meets a new
patient, it is presumed that the work will
be about what has happened in the past.
But life does not pause while the treatment
proceeds. And sometimes what happens
while the therapy is progressing ends up
changing everything. I didn't know that
the door I was about to open would be to a
remarkable life, the most difficult passage of which I was destined and privileged
to share.

I approached Lillie's room as a nurse came shuffling out, her head shaking back and forth. When she saw me about to go in, she said with a forced smile, "Good luck." Not knowing what to expect, I entered and found Lillie sitting next to the far wall in a wheelchair. The staff had told me that she was a handful. She had suffered a stroke in the left hemisphere of her brain, which had left her right arm and leg very weak.

"Good morning, Lillie." I said. "I'm Doctor Sabine."

Lillie scowled at me but said nothing.

"I am a psychologist, and your doctor asked me to see you. Whenever someone comes to the hospital because of a stroke, I am asked to do an evaluation. I want to do a little testing with you, so I can see how your brain is working right now. When we are finished, I will make recommendations to the treatment team to see if we can help you recover faster.

She continued her angry stare. She slowly began to look at me and shake her head, as if saying "no."

"No," I asked.

She shook her head again.

Confused, I asked, "You are saying you don't want me to evaluate you?"

Her eyes narrowed and a smile, made one-sided by her stroke, suggested I was making the correct interpretation. Lillie was obviously aphasic, unable to speak normally because of damage to the speech center of her brain. She appeared strong-willed and independent, but she struggled with the challenge of not being able to express herself. Still, with her feisty determination, she had managed to run off every therapist who had tried to convince her to go to therapy.

"Lillie, I have worked with people who have had strokes for several years now. One of the toughest things to deal with is the loss of the ability to speak."

"Y....Es!" was her response.

I explained my evaluation would only last a few minutes. She rolled her eyes, but I took that as permission to proceed. It was clear that her stroke had been significant. She was able to comprehend what people said and she understood what was going on around her, but her expressive speech continued to fail her.

The evaluation was brief, typical when aphasia is present. Because the testing is comprised of mostly verbal tasks, the evaluation didn't take long. When I was finished, I put away my materials and sat back in my chair.

"Thank you for your help with that. I know it was tedious."

She looked relieved to be able to stop searching for the right word and rest for a minute, and I asked her if she'd like to go outside for some fresh air.

I rolled Lillie out to the little courtyard in the back of the hospital and we sat out in the warm spring sun for a while. I didn't say anything much, but she seemed to enjoy being outside. She sat with her eyes closed, soaking in the sun. Her earlier anger seemed to have drained away.

After a few minutes, I rolled her back inside. When we got back to the room, she reached out with her left hand and touched my arm. I stopped and looked down at her.

"Th-th-th-th." She tried several times to say something, and I could see her frustration ignite. She furrowed her brow and gritted her teeth.

"Lillie, are you trying to thank me?" I asked.

She let out a sigh and nodded, the stress draining from her face.

"Well, if the weather is nice tomorrow, maybe we could go out again."

And again, she smiled.

A "cardiovascular accident," commonly called a stroke, is a cruel thief, often robbing a person of abilities we take for granted. A stroke slices willy-nilly through the brain, destroying connections from one neuron to another and corrupting connections within our lives and what we hold dear.

For instance, a stroke can take away words like "tomato," "car," or "table," even though we have always known what these objects were called. A stroke sometimes steals precious identifiers, like the names of our children or spouse, as if we had never heard them before. Things we knew inherently just a few hours before are suddenly irretrievable.

During my first practicum placement at the Veteran's Administration hospital in Louisville, Kentucky, I was evaluating a man who had suffered a left-hemisphere stroke. I asked him if he knew the name of the continent where the Sahara Desert is located. I could see his jaw tense as he looked at me. His mouth opened, but he was unable to get the answer out. He growled his frustration.

"You know the answer, don't you?" I said.

"Yes, I do," he replied.

"But you can't say it."

He tried to say it again with no luck.

I handed him a notepad and asked him if he thought he would be more successful writing the word. Even though he was right-handed, he took the pen in his left hand, as the stroke had made his right hand useless, at least for the time being. Still, the word would not come to him.

I was ready to retrieve the pad from him and continue with something else, but he gestured for me to wait. He began to touch the pen to the paper. In dismay, I watched him draw an easily recognizable outline of the continent of Africa—with his *non*-dominant hand! This man, who had sat and conversed with me rather well during the evaluation, had lost names and simple words for things in such a strangely circumscribed way.

Although they are sometimes fatal, strokes at other times are vicious, or mischievous, or relentless. While one patient might suffer severe impairments that resolve quickly, sometimes in a few days with or without therapy, another might have relatively mild deficits that remain agonizingly constant, regardless of how much treatment is undertaken.

Patients have told me repeatedly about their experience when they first realize they have suffered a stroke. They usually meet the news with confusion. *What has happened to me? Why can't I move my hand? Why am I crying when I am not sad? Why can't I see the way I used to?*

Whatever the particular symptoms or deficits, the patient has a hard time accepting the strange reality that life has suddenly changed for the worse.

When the initial shock has subsided, some of the afflicted are temporarily filled with gratitude. *I survived. I could have died, but I am still here. I have cheated death for the time being.*

Before long, however, the fact that the symptoms are not going away, that they will persist at least for a period of time, sinks in. Then, the chronic apprehension starts. *When will I be able to speak again, or swallow my own food, or walk? What if I never get better? What will life be like for me from now on?*

Research suggests that the majority of people who have a stroke will go through a significant struggle with depression. Given the devastation a stroke wields, this is not surprising. Beyond the existential challenges that might bring on depression, the stroke itself seems to disrupt the chemistry of the brain, directly causing the condition. Other symptoms mimicking psychiatric disorders may appear. Some stroke victims may hallucinate or become paranoid. Some may have rapid onset disorientation and memory problems, going from normal one day to having dementia the next.

The combinations of impairments are seemingly infinite. I have seen thousands of people in the days immediately following their stroke, and I still routinely see new symptom constellations. For Lillie, the two factors that were enduring, with terrible tenacity, were her inability to walk safely and her expressive aphasia, her inability to speak.

Walking was unsafe because of weakness, her substantial weight, and her unreliable equilibrium. She was sometimes unsteady on her feet and dizzy. Therefore, the wheelchair went with her everywhere.

Lillie's speech was easily her greatest aggravation. She could say a word from time to time. Sometimes, she was well into a sentence before she would come to an abrupt halt, blocked by an agonizingly simple word she simply wasn't able to iterate. The fact that she had almost finished the sentence made the failure even worse.

One word she was able to say without fail was my name, David. She said it often, and I came to love the sound of her saying it.

When we first met, she tried several times to say "Dr. Sabine." My last name is hard for most people to pronounce, but it was impossible for Lillie. Finally, as if asking permission to refer to me by my first name, she said "David" with a rising inflection.

"Please call me David," I said. "In fact, that would make me very happy."

"David," she said, smiling.

"Perfect," I responded.

"David," she repeated.

Another problem some patients have after a stroke is connecting the affect or emotion they feel to their speech. The sound of their voice flattens and sounds almost robotic. This was not the case with Lillie. After a while, she became quite skilled at saying many different things by simply repeating my name. She could say "thank you," or "please." She could express pride in me, frustration with me, along with a host of feelings like surprise, fear, sorrow, pain, and joy merely by the inflection in her voice when she said "David."

The fact that my name had become a touchstone for Lillie to her interior life had a powerful effect upon me. As I said earlier, therapists are often moved with a desire to fix or rescue their patients. This was a powerful pull for me when it came to Lillie. I wanted desperately to free her to speak with me, to enjoy the full complement of vocabulary with which to relate her feelings. But in our early work together, she had one reliable word to convey it all: David.

Over the course of her hospital stay, Lillie and I went outside several times. Mostly, we just sat together. I would tell her any story that came to mind and talk about my hopes for her recovery. The use of her hand and leg was progressing slowly, but improvement in her speech remained elusive. When she was discharged about three weeks later, she had no more functional speech than when she had been admitted. I suspected she would find the adjustment to life after the hospital difficult, but I also saw her strong determination. She would not be defeated easily.

Two weeks later, when I arrived at my office and picked up my schedule, I saw Lillie's name on it. That was surprising, because we had not made a plan for follow-up appointments after she was discharged from the hospital. I asked my office manager how the appointment had been made, knowing that Lillie had a hard time speaking. She said Lillie's son, Pat, had called on her behalf.

As I waited for Lillie to arrive, I was apprehensive. I wasn't sure how to proceed with psychotherapy under the circumstances. How would I get to know her better if she couldn't speak?

In this, I underestimated her. She had already figured this out. Lillie came into my office pushed in her wheelchair by a slender man who appeared to be in his forties. Lillie smiled when she saw me and pointed over her shoulder.

"P-p-p-p- at."

"Oh, this is your son, Pat," I said.

She nodded vigorously.

"Pat, it is a pleasure to meet you," I said.

Pat didn't look up or acknowledge me. He closed the door on his way out to wait for her. Lillie looked embarrassed at Pat's behavior. She said something that sounded like "scissor-friends-in-ya," which I repeated. She shook her head and said again "scissor-friends-in-ya," I was still confused, and she made the universal sign for loopy or crazy, circling her index finger around her temple.

"Oh," I said, "Schizophrenia! You're saying Pat has Schizophrenia!"

Lillie's laugh gave way to a sigh as she nodded her head. She half-shut her eyes in a squint, and when she opened them, she nodded again as tears welled up.

"I'm so sorry, Lillie," I said empathically. "That must be hard for you to see Pat struggle like that."

She nodded, took a deep breath, and appeared to be ready to move along with the session.

The problem was that I had no idea how to proceed. I knew I could find something to say. But how was I to know and understand Lillie?

"Lillie, how do we do this?" I asked. "Usually, psychotherapy is like a conversation, a conversation about your life. But your aphasia makes it hard for you to share your story with me."

Lillie put her hand on a cloth bag she held on her lap. I had not noticed it until she pointed it out.

She held it up and offered it to me. By the weight, I figured that the bag held books of some kind.

She nodded when I asked her if she wanted me to open it.

I untied the drawstring and pulled out what appeared to be several hand-written journals. I opened the first one. A dedication was inscribed on the yellowed first page in elegant, legible strokes. "This book is dedicated to my dear, gentle father, who wanted to be remembered."

Lillie's plan for us sank in. "Perfect," I said with a smile. "I guess you have found a way to share your story with me. If you want to leave them with me, I will read them before our next session."

Lillie shook her head, "N-n-n-o-o-o-o-w-w-w."

"Even better," I replied.

Sharing the journals was a great idea. I would read them out loud in Lillie's presence. In doing so, Lillie would be able to share the thoughtful narrative of her life with me. She would just use my voice to do it.

"You want to start right now?" I asked.

Lillie closed her eyes and leaned her head back, smiling. Turning the page, I cleared my throat and began.

"April 15, 1861, Abraham Lincoln issued a call for 75,000 state militia—and the Civil War had begun. Lincoln was a native of Springfield, Illinois, and about 150 miles south was McCleansboro, Illinois. This was the Hamilton county seat and the home of Isaac Duvalls."

With this short paragraph the journal captured my imagination. Lillie smiled faintly, eyes still closed, as I read. The reading was for Lillie's benefit, but I confess I found myself absorbed by the powerful narrative.

The journal had all the qualities of great story-telling—tension, adventure, humor, and occasional horror. Early in the family history, stories had been passed down through a sort of informal oral tradition. Lillie brought these tales to the page for select people to enjoy. I read especially eagerly the episodes that sounded like they came from a classic Western movie.

In one event, an Indian raid while the men were away, the little family dog had to be suffocated to prevent it from barking and revealing the place where her ancestors were hiding in a ravine, watching the Indians ransack and plunder their home. Another tale was about her father as a fourteen-year-old run-away, spending days hopping trains, eating only what was given to him by the good will of strangers and the occasional watermelon that fell to the tracks. He befriended native Apaches and was witness to their elderly Chief, Geronimo, riding his paint pony many times. Lillie, always the good journalist, "fact-checked" this rather interesting detail and found that, indeed, Geronimo lived out his later years near Fort Sill, Oklahoma, and would have been about 70 when her father saw him.

The Civil War was a major theme of the family history. Stories she recounted were about friends and family who had fought and were wounded in the battles, by the actual bullets of their "Yankee" brothers or by the memories of what they had witnessed. Lillie did not avoid the darker aspects of the Civil War era. She recounted how shortly after the war, citizens believed to be Yankee sympathizers were rounded up and hanged, even though the war was officially over. One friend of her family relayed a message about "feeling bad" because he had dragged a boy out from under his parents' bed and hanged him in the front yard with his mother looking on.

A heritage of faith also emerged, and several men in Lillie's family, including her paternal grandfather, entered the ministry. Some were "circuit-riding" preachers who served several congregations, traveling between churches on horse-back.

Lillie's grandfather died of typhoid fever at the age of 28, leaving her grandmother with small children to feed. At his funeral, pioneer families and Indians alike came forward to the coffin and placed money on it to support the widow and her boys.

Periodically, I came to a part of a story where Lillie had recorded an aside, reflecting on what she had just rendered.

"Hard to picture life as it was 80 years ago. Sometimes, it seems unreal that my mother and daddy could have lived some of their lives a hundred years ago—for they seem so near to me. Time really does fly—like a vapor that appears for a short time and is gone."

Lillie was born on March 8, 1913. Her memories and anecdotes of her early years were tenderly delivered, especially her memories of her daddy, who was a fur trader. She hunted and fished with him, and she fondly recalled sitting at his feet while he played the fiddle for her. Her mother was an equally hard worker, for years running a hamburger stand in Jacksboro, Texas.

Reading about her early years was like reading a first-hand account of an all-American childhood. She went to school, played baseball with the boys, got a job at the "picture show," won spelling contests and was chosen as a cheerleader, all in the shadow of World War I. She went to college, an unprecedented event in her family. Because this was during the Great Depression, this achievement was even more markedly exceptional.

When Lillie described going to college, she included a photo of herself at 18-years-old. That picture moves me to this day. She was wearing a simple sleeveless dress and a small pendant around her neck. Her smile seemed effortless as she looked into the camera. The most remarkable feature was her eyes, revealing intelligence, passion, confidence and determination.

As I looked at the photo and compared it to the 82-year-old woman in the wheelchair before me, I recognized the same look. Lillie's appetite for life had remained steadfast. Even her willingness to engage in psychotherapy at her age was an indicator that she did not accept life's destiny passively. When she was called to exit the stage, she was going to have some input into how it went. To borrow a metaphor from her beloved sport, baseball, she was going to go down swinging. She did not know how to give up.

When Lillie was seventeen, the idyllic days of youth and innocence were abruptly behind her. Her first love, Otis Reedy, the "man of her dreams," was killed in an automobile accident. They had loved each other deeply, and after he died, Lillie learned that he had desired to marry her.

After the shock of this loss, Lillie struggled. She dated another young man, Rufus, but they never committed to each other. He married another girl, but some time later, he took his own life. Rufus's sister told her that he had often voiced his regret over not marrying Lillie.

Lillie found her way out of sorrows in an unusual way, playing softball. She learned about a softball league in Wichita Falls, and she was soon playing on more than one team. She joined a team that traveled all over the United States, competing against the best female players in the country. The story of Lillie and her team's accomplishments was chronicled in a 1996 article in the Wichita Falls Times Record News.

Lillie spent her spare time with her softball teammates, but she also worked for her Uncle Hobbs in his fast-growing auto parts business. When Uncle Hobbs and his partner, Mr. Duncan, divided the business, Lillie went to work for Mr. Duncan. While working there, she met her future husband, Phillip. After a brief engagement, they were married. Lillie's first baby, Susan, was born a year later. Susan was soon joined by a baby brother, Mike.

Lillie's journal took digressions from time to time. In one digression, she talked about the U.S. presidencies she had lived through, commenting on each. She had met Gerald Ford and shaken his hand. Never one to be shy about her own opinion, she was non-partisan in her displeasures, not caring much for either Jimmy Carter or Ronald Reagan. She was bitterly opposed to the first Gulf War, believing the war to be more about George H. W. Bush's ego than anything else. She also recounted seeing Jack Dempsey and Helen Keller, and meeting Amelia Earhart.

Throughout the readings, we stopped many times to cry, laugh, or take a moment for Lillie to add to the story. Her speech returned somewhat, although she would never recover it entirely. After several sessions of reading, the journal abruptly concluded. The last, two-line entry chilled me and caused Lillie to break down in tears.

"I hope to finish my story later. Susan's brain aneurysm March 13, 1991 has almost killed my desire to write. This is the worst thing I've ever had to face."

This entry referred to Susan, the oldest of her four children. Susan had died from the aneurysm. She had become Lillie's source of both physical and emotional support as she became more age-impaired. She was also her confidante and best friend. Lillie had a particularly hard time pronouncing the name because of the aphasia, but often, by the time she managed to say "Susan," she was crying.

Lillie certainly had known sorrow. She had lost her "first true love" when she was only seventeen. Her parents had died. In 1988, Phillip, her husband of many years, died also. But those losses, while painful, did not devastate her like the death of Susan.

I never fully understood the dynamics of her marriage to Phillip. Lillie did speak at one point about "when I stopped loving Phillip." She and Phillip had owned their own auto parts store for years. By the 1960's, they were relatively well off, although not wealthy. With her experience in bookkeeping, Lillie had begun to notice that sales were high, but the cash flow didn't reflect it. She did some searching and found tens of thousands of dollars under a bed, where Phillip had been squirreling the money away. His explanation was "I was afraid you were going to spend all of our money on the kids."

I still don't know a lot about Lillie's feelings for Phillip. She rarely spoke about his death. However, by the time she came to see me, tragedy had begun its relentless assault and maybe Phillip was simply overshadowed.

Like Lillie, I have been blessed with four children. When my first child, Lauren, was born nearly 30 years ago, I carried her over to the corner of the delivery room and introduced myself to her. Tears of both joy and relief rolled down my face, joy that she was here and relief she was okay. But, they were also tears of fear. With the arrival of Lauren Elizabeth, my world and my role in it had suddenly changed. I had long been fearful of pain and death, but now I was vulnerable to pain that would be inconceivable if something were to happen to this beautiful child, who was now my charge. I was her protector, and only with my own death would I reluctantly relinquish that job.

When I work with parents who have lost a child, I try to focus on the patients and their grief. I don't dare shift to thinking about losing Lauren, Ryan, Abby, or Ben. I can't bear it.

So, when Lillie's journal ended with Susan's death, I understood why she stopped writing. Everything had stopped at the edge of that terrible loss.

"Lillie," I said, "I am so sorry about Susan. I can tell that it was devastating."

Lillie squeezed her eyes tightly and began trying to say something.

"Mmmmm . . . " Her furrowed brow and bowed head seemed to express agony.

"Take your time, Lillie. Take all the time you need."

"Mmmmm . . ike," she said, and burst into a sob.

Lillie was trying to tell me that Mike, her eldest son, was gone, too. In his youth, Mike was the rebel, the prototypical "greaser." In spite of a conservative religious upbringing, he had rejected that path and finally ended up mired in alcoholism. In recent months, Mike had changed paths again, seeming like he might find real hope and recovery. He had moved in with Lillie and had found the courage to cobble together a full month of sobriety.

Lillie said she hadn't known what to think when that first month was over, having been disappointed so many other times. Mike had worried her so much and for so long. So many times, she had let herself entertain hope for him, only to see him relapse. She had finally become distrustful of hope's chicanery. But Mike had said goodbye to his former drinking buddies and was staying out of the bar. He and Lillie, distanced from one another by the incompatibility of his choices and her unwavering values, had begun to build a bridge.

Then, just as Lillie was beginning to entertain the fickle company of hope one more time, just as she and her son found a shelter in one another, she discovered him one morning collapsed on the floor with a heart attack. In shock and desperation, she called 911 and gathered him in her arms, but it was too late. Mike, too, was gone, just a year after Susan.

My mind was unable to calculate this loss on top of Susan's death. It suddenly became clearer why Lillie had suffered her brutal stroke. Her body simply could not hold together under the weight of these losses.

I am the first to confess that I don't know what to say that can help in the face of such grief. I wish I were wise enough to share something that would make a difference. But I have learned that words don't help much. I do my best to offer my presence and not pull back from the pain, even if I have nothing to say.

Lillie and I spent the ensuing months struggling with these two losses. We talked about the joy she'd found in Susan and how much she had depended on her. We spoke of her pride in the changes Mike had been making. We also talked about her beloved brother, with whom she had always been competitive, and who had recently taken his own life.

But, at least she had Pat. Because Lillie was distant from her other daughter, she relied upon Pat to bring her to her sessions with me. He always brought a giant volume of classic literature or history with him and read in the waiting room until it was time to load her up for home.

Pat was a remarkable character in his own right. He was a freelance photographer and was renowned for his brilliance. At the age of fifteen, when he started to show signs of what would ultimately be diagnosed as Schizophrenia, Pat was sent to military school in the hopes that his rather unusual rebellions would be channeled in a more productive manner.

No one knew that Pat's behavior was not youthful rebellion, but an early manifestation of psychosis and paranoia. Military school was not the solution to corralling his bizarre and random passions.

Pat was hard to control. He was known to take off on a whim and hitchhike across the country. Lillie told me about a time Pat had absconded with the family car and gotten half way across the country before anyone caught up with him.

As I watched her interact with Pat from week to week, I could see the tender way that Lillie, normally not one to "suffer fools lightly," would tolerate Pat's eccentricities. Sometimes she lost patience, especially in social situations where she found his behavior embarrassing. But generally, I could see how much she loved and protected him as he tenderly met her needs as best he could. In spite of the complicated nature of their relationship, she was grateful for his company. Odd as he was, he seemed to offer consolation in the otherwise desolate landscape of loss.

Contrary to what might be expected in such deep grief, our sessions were not filled with tears. Lillie, for all of her pain, loved to laugh. I heard that she even laughed heartily in the limousine that took her to the cemetery after Mike's funeral, when someone recalled an amusing story about him that she found humorous.

In a few months, Lillie's speech gradually returned, and she took firm control of our sessions. She wanted to decide what we talked about, and I was happy to let her. The destination was always interesting. She worked diligently in exploring her grief, and I also learned much more detail about her life.

Lillie was deeply religious, and faith was a matter of upmost importance. She attended the Church of Christ. At 37, she earned her degree in business. She loved Jimmie Connors and John Elway. Lillie was highly competitive, and she would be furious if someone solved the puzzle before her when watching Wheel of Fortune. She was stern, loyal, and principled. She loved to travel. She had been all over the United States and had even toured through Europe. All these insights rounded out my understanding of this remarkable life.

One day, Lillie seemed to be in a mood to talk about our relationship.

"David, it has been a few years now, hasn't it, that we have worked together?"

"Yes, Lillie," I said, "It has been a rare privilege for me."

"Well, you have become very important to me," she said. "You helped me so much after losing Susan and Mike. I can't thank you enough, really. But I have something I would like to ask of you, if you are willing."

"What is it?" I asked.

"Well, I am an old lady now," she said, in a rare reference to her age, "and it has always been important to me how I will be remembered. I know you were a minister in the years before you became a psychologist. I was wondering if you would be willing to deliver my funeral address when the time comes."

I was deeply moved by this request, but I didn't know what to say. One of the sacrosanct principles of psychotherapy is to keep the relationship pure and protected. Only on rare occasions and only for specific therapeutic goals would anything happen outside the structure and boundary of the therapy office. A therapist does not go to dinner or have a drink with a client. The therapist does not socialize or do business with the client. Most obvious, the therapist avoids any romantic or sexual relations with a client.

But what would I do about Lillie's request? It was certainly unusual. I felt I knew the source of her request. She wanted to be known, to be remembered. She needed to share the experiences and beliefs about life that had compelled her to record her memoir.

The last chapters of that story had not been put down on paper. The written record had been truncated by Susan's death and it would never again be penned. But, the narrative had to be completed in some way. Having it told was of utmost importance to Lillie.

Susan and Mike were gone. Pat was limited because of his illness. And she had a conflicted relationship with her other daughter. Lillie lacked someone to help her continue the narrative; more and more, I was becoming the sole witness to Lillie's telling of her story.

Our therapy work had revolved around this narrative of her life. Now, because of a series of tragedies, Lillie seemed to be entrusting me with completing the story for her. She wanted me to be the one who would someday carry her legend to posterity. I couldn't help but be moved by the honor implicit in her request.

That, however, did not mitigate the fact that accepting Lillie's request might change our relationship. Would that mean a dual relationship? Was I tacitly becoming her minister too? Probably so.

On the other hand, when Lillie was no longer living, the issue of a dual relationship would be moot. Technically, I suppose, the relationship would be over at that point. But it really wasn't that simple. Would she behave differently if I were in a way now becoming her biographer? Would she be less open, less disclosing?

It was not lost on me that psychotherapy is usually a private affair, and though I had been a witness to many lives and stories through the years, no one had asked me to step out from behind that protection and speak publicly about his or her life. Then again, Lillie was not like anyone I had ever met.

I decided to talk very frankly with her about my reservations. When I finally finished, I noticed a sparkle in her eyes and a hint of a smile on her face.

"David," she said tenderly. "You know me better than any person alive. Do you think I am going to be less than candid with you or relate to you differently just because I asked you to speak for me at my funeral?"

I smiled. She was right. Lillie had her own opinions. She had never been shy about speaking them plainly. It was unlikely she would start now.

"Okay, Lillie. I will do it. I would be honored to do it."

"Thank you, David," Lillie said, still smiling.

Over the next few months, Lillie's health began to decline. I was grieved to see the unmistakable assault of debility and disintegration. Lillie was a fighter, but time is a formidable opponent and we all ultimately succumb, no matter how resolutely we resist.

Time is a formidable opponent and we all ultimately succumb, no matter how resolutely we resist.

Lillie's health problems soon required more supervision and support than Pat was able to provide, regardless of his best efforts. The decision was made that Lillie needed skilled nursing care, and she moved to a local nursing home that was owned and run by the Church of Christ.

Neither Lillie nor Pat found this change to be easy. From my first encounter with her, I had known that Lillie was not going to be a good candidate for institutional care. She had been a difficult patient after her stroke, and the nursing home staff found her equally challenging. She had been a lifelong closet feminist, and her fierce, demanding autonomy was not amenable to the role of "good patient."

Lillie's attending physician wrote an order so that I could continue therapy with her at her bedside. I did my best to assist her in adjusting to the challenge of this new accommodation and to help the staff learn how best to work with her.

I did not anticipate how hard this transition would be for Pat. His mother was his anchor and his protector from inner demons. She was also his reason for living. I regret that I was not aware or insightful enough to anticipate how this transition would be for him.

One week, I came to the nursing home to see Lillie for our regular session. When I walked into the room, I found several family members, including grandchildren, at her bedside. Lillie was in tears. "Oh, David," and sobbed uncontrollably when she saw me.

I saw that the people in the room had their tear-filled eyes directed at the floor.

"What has happened?" I implored.

"It's Pat," one of them said.

I looked back to Lillie. She had that unmistakable look of a mother swallowed in pain and grief.

In an instant, I felt an intense and fulminating anger well up. The feeling was so immediate that I almost had to leave the room. Something had happened to Pat. How could that be? Weren't the deaths of Susan and Mike enough? Shouldn't there be some kind of limit on the grief that any one person has to endure?

My composure failed me and tears ran down my face. Without knowing any more details about Pat, I leaned over Lillie's bed and put my arms around her. "Oh, David," she sobbed again and again.

"I am so sorry, Lillie," I said, bereft of anything else to say.

The family shared with me the story that was too grim to be true, but too true to be denied. After Lillie had gone to the nursing home, Pat had become more and more reclusive. Apparently, his paranoia began running unchecked. He had become obsessed with the debt he was carrying on a couple of credit cards. His worry about how he was going to pay them off had become malignant. He became delusional and believed that the people he owed were conspiring to make him pay, and would soon come to carry him off to exact in torture the payment he was unable to make.

In his solitude, the delusions and fear had become intolerable. Pat decided that he had to take things into his own hands. He found a lock-blade knife and tried to stab himself to end the torture, but he was unsuccessful in applying enough force to do the job. In desperation, he grabbed a large butcher knife and climbed up on his dining room table. He jumped off the table onto the knife, but only succeeded in stabbing himself. Unbelievably, no doubt more afraid and bleeding badly, he climbed back onto the table and jumped again. This time, Pat was successful with his objective. Alone, ensconced in his home and incarcerated by his psychosis, Lillie's youngest child and troubled boy died.

That day, I stayed with Lillie for a long time. Toward the end of my visit, Lillie looked up at me. I had encountered the face of sorrow many times in my work as a therapist and, before that, as a minister, but I had never witnessed the despair I beheld in Lillie's countenance.

Her grief was like a powerful riptide, relentless and irresistible, carrying her spirit and hope farther and farther out to sea.

"Lillie," I said, "I'll stay with you for a while. If you want, we can talk about Pat, or we *cannot* talk about Pat. We can talk about anything you want to. Or we can sit here and not talk at all. I just want you to know I am here with you. We have come a long way together, and I will be here with you through this."

I was rambling, trying too hard. I so wanted to help, but I was outside of a wall of grief so strong that my words were nothing but muted shoutings into a howling wind. I could not go with her. God help me, I didn't have the courage to go with her, even if I could.

I dragged a chair up to her bedside there in the nursing home, and we waited in silence. *For what*? I had no idea. After what seemed like a long time, Lillie reached her hand above the rail of the bed and I took it in mine.

"David," she said through the tears, "would you do something for me?"

"What is it, Lillie" I said, "If I can, I will."

"Would you be willing to say a few words at Pat's funeral?"

Honestly, I had not foreseen such a request. I knew that Lillie had a strong faith, and I really didn't know Pat very well. I assumed that Lillie would have clergy she would want to call.

Gently, I reminded her how important it was to protect the privacy and confidentiality of our relationship.

Lillie persisted. "David," she implored, "if you are willing, I really would like for you to do this. No one really understood Pat. He lived very privately with his illness, and you understand it so much better that anyone else I know. You could help everyone see the meaning in his rather odd, unconventional life."

Even in grief, Lillie was tenacious. At that moment, perhaps out of weakness, perhaps out of a fantasy of being able to rescue her, I simply agreed.

"Lillie, it would be an honor to speak up for Pat."

A few days later, Lillie, her family, and I gathered at a simple grave-side service. I stood up and spoke about Pat. I recommended him to eternity and the memories of his family.

When the brief service was over, I went to Lillie's side. She was moving tentatively, pushing her walker. Suddenly, she stopped and looked down.

Following her gaze, I realized she was looking at her own grave, where she would soon be buried. I wondered what she was thinking.

It is difficult to contemplate one's own mortality, but I suspected she might have a great deal of ambivalence about living on, infirm, and alone most of the time in a nursing home bed, mourning three lost children. I suspected she was probably ready to go.

Looking up at me, she said, "David, thank you. You will never know what it meant to me to have you speak for Pat."

"Thank you, Lillie, for the chance to do it," I said.

"And you are still going to do the same for me, right? We have a deal?"

"Yes Lillie, we have a deal."

And with that, we went back to the car, and back to our lives.

Over the next few months, Lillie weakened, whether due to her medical problems or the weight of her grief. One day, I got a call telling me that Lillie had died. Without a great deal of physical pain, she had finally slipped away.

In keeping with my promise, I presided over her funeral service and delivered her eulogy. As I admired her family that day, I noted all of Lillie's beautiful and handsome grandchildren. I smiled, thinking about how she loved them all, recalling how she wanted them to know about their grandmother. As I spoke that day, I did my best to summarize Lillie's remarkable life.

Through the years, I have performed many rites of passage—baptisms, weddings, and funerals. Sometimes the services have been hard to do. But Lillie's was a joy. I relished in telling about such a rich and interesting life. I think she would have been pleased.

`But what I could not say, what only I knew, was the personal affection I had for Lillie as her therapist. I had the chance to traverse some of the most important and painful passages of her life with her. I was privy to the heroic way she had wrestled and fought, squeezing every last drop of sweetness from her life despite her grief and loss. It was a rare privilege, one to which I refer often and fondly even after all these years.

Lillie, thank you for sharing your life so courageously with me. I am ever richer for it. Because you came to me unable to speak, I thought that it would be fitting to close in your own words. Below is an entry from your journal. I want you to know that I will always remember you. Wherever you are, Godspeed, my dear friend.

"This is a simple book, written so my mother and daddy, and my brother and I will be remembered. I hope as these words are read by my 'great' or 'great-great' grandchildren, you will know how I loved life and loved you and would have loved to see you grow up. I hope you will say, 'I wish I had known my great-great grandma Lillie Blacklock.'"

chapter three

ONCE TO DIE

Life is a near-death experience.
   —Dr. John

IN THE FALL of my fortieth year, I heard Death clear his throat, as if he were about to call my name. It is sometimes said that a little knowledge is dangerous. The Wednesday morning before Thanksgiving, 1998, a little knowledge was what got me in trouble.

In the middle of the morning over the previous few days, I had struggled with a transient dizziness as I sat in my office working. I couldn't tell why I was having this symptom at the same time each day.

On that particular Wednesday, I had gotten up early to see Lorna, a 91-year-old woman who was a new patient at the rehab hospital. I was to evaluate her for suspected anxiety. When I entered her room about seven, I found her sitting up in bed staring blankly at her breakfast.

"Good morning, Lorna," I said. "I am Dr. Sabine. I am a psychologist, and your doctors here thought you might be a little worried these last few days."

Lorna tentatively agreed.

"Well, would you be willing to tell me about your worries?" She reached her frail hand to the top of her simple nightgown and pulled it down slightly. There, on the left side of her chest below her collar-bone, was a two-inch long, finely-sutured incision that sat atop a device implanted under her skin. Lorna had a new pacemaker.

"Having this thing in my body is really worrying me. It's so weird. It's not me, but it's in me."

I spent the next few minutes getting acquainted with Lorna and talking about what having a device implanted in her body meant to her. Before I left, I taught her a simple relaxation exercise to help manage her anxiety and promised to return after the Thanksgiving holiday with more techniques that I thought would be helpful.

After I bade her goodbye, I rushed back to the office. I had a full schedule that Wednesday morning, especially since I was taking the afternoon off for the holiday.

I looked at my schedule to see that my next patient was Daniel, a quiet, sad, ten-year-old boy who had been seeing me for a short while. His mother had brought Daniel to see me after his father had been killed by a drunk driver in a car accident. For three sessions I had struggled to reach him but had been unsuccessful. He was locked away in grief, and he had so far refused to let me in. My desire to respect Daniel's own process for grieving the death of his father was at war with my concern that he was having trouble sleeping and was losing weight. His doctor had prescribed an anti-depressant medication, which Daniel's mother had given him faithfully for a month, to no discernible effect.

The early loss of a parent has been called "the wound that never heals," and so far, it seemed the case with Daniel. His father had been a beloved physician in town, but he had never let his busy practice stop him from putting his only child first. Daniel's mother described the bond between her husband and her son as amazing. Dad had been at every soccer game, piano recital, and PTA program. On occasion, he'd take Daniel camping, just the two of them. Every night, he carried Daniel to bed by piggyback. But beyond faithful attendance at all of Daniel's activities, her husband sat

There had been a sacredness of purpose they shared, and whatever they were going to encounter would be taken on with passion and diligence.

together with her son at breakfast time with identical, intent countenances. The big one would ponder a day filled with caring for patients and the little one would consider his spelling test and whether to ride his bike to school or walk.

There had been a sacredness of purpose they shared, and whatever they were going to encounter would be taken on with passion and diligence. On those idyllic mornings, before Death broke down the door, their home was a shelter and a sanctuary from pain, ringed by a charm and incantation that made the love and peace they shared impenetrable.

There had been no way for her to cushion the blow for Daniel. She told me that her own grief had been unimaginably devastating, but the worst part by far was having to wake up Daniel to tell him his sweet father was gone. She had stood in shock outside his bedroom door that morning, unable to make her feet move, knowing what the next few minutes held. Trying to keep her sobbing from waking him, she had knelt down to compose herself. *God, how can I do this? This can't be happening. This can't be real. Please wake me up from all of this.*

She had spent a few minutes outside his door, digging her fingernails into her palms to try to distract her from her heartrending pain. With her hand shaking, she slowly pushed Daniel's door open and saw his still, sleeping form under his covers. She knew that after the next few moments, his life would never be the same.

I wanted so badly to reach Daniel. He was caving in on himself and shutting out the world. He was not irritable or oppositional. But he answered my questions blankly, usually in one syllable words. He wasn't able to find his way out of the dark.

That morning, as the session was winding down, I sat in the office in silence. A warm fire glowed in the fireplace, but Daniel, eyes downcast, paid it no attention. The session had been completely unsuccessful as far as I could tell. Every attempt to engage, distract, or approach him had been stymied by his disarming pain. I stared at the fire, at a loss as to what to say or do that might allow Daniel to open himself up.

Just then, the dizziness that had been bothering me about this time each of the last few days washed over me. I hoped Daniel wouldn't sense my distress. He did not need me to pass out for no apparent reason. That disturbing possibility snapped me back to the moment.

I concentrated on the ceramic fireplace log as I tried to ride it out. Suddenly, I entertained the idea that maybe there was a connection between the fire and my lightheadedness. My fireplace was relatively new. In the middle of a renovation the previous year, workers had stripped out plaster from an interior wall and come upon a fireplace long hidden by an earlier remodeling. They reclaimed the hearth, built out a new mantle, and installed a gas fireplace with ceramic logs. We were in the middle of an Arctic surge that occasionally blows through North Texas, and of late I was lighting the fireplace each morning to chase away the chill.

I wondered if that fireplace was the reason I was dizzy. What if I was slowly poisoning myself with carbon monoxide? Maybe the fireplace was not properly vented. I certainly had noticed a strong smell of gas, and I knew that carbon monoxide could accumulate in the body over time, and that one day, after multiple discreet exposures, a person can just fall over dead!

I brought the frustrating session with Daniel to an end, no progress in sight. I'd resume where we'd left off in our next session the following week. Wishing him and his mother the impossible, a happy Thanksgiving holiday, I still couldn't shake the worry about a connection between the fireplace and my dizziness.

After they drove off, I decided to walk the short block between my office and the hospital to get checked out for carbon monoxide poisoning. I was only moments away from a brush with death for another condition entirely, but I didn't know it then.

I told the ER staff about my dizziness and my suspicion about the fireplace gas, also mentioning my mild chest pain and feeling that my blood pressure was high. I was ushered to a treatment room for a blood gas test, which would determine if I was suffering from carbon monoxide poisoning. First, I drank a Lidocaine elixir to address possible indigestion, which might be the cause of my chest pain. Next, I was hooked up to an ECG to monitor my heart. Then, to address my blood pressure, I had a nitroglycerin tablet placed under my tongue. I was left alone for a while, resting on an exam table that was tilted to elevate my head.

In good time, a nurse came in to administer the blood gas test. She explained it was more uncomfortable than a regular method of drawing blood from a vein. She needed to draw blood from an artery, which is deeper and harder to locate than a vein. She was going to insert a needle deep into my wrist, and she warned me to lie still to increase the likelihood that we could get this done with one stick.

I have always had an issue with needles, and this little lecture left me quite unsettled. She prepped the site and poised the needle. As she began to push the needle my world went black.

When we sleep, we have a sense that some time has passed, even though we are not aware of it elapsing the same way we are during our waking moments. But when we pass out, the time we have lost is nowhere in our awareness. However long we were unconscious, the moment we awaken is the very next moment in time.

When I passed out, one nurse was attending to me. When I awoke, I was in a scene from "ER," an old television medical drama. There were at least eight people standing over me, all with very serious looks on their faces. A man was staring intently at the tape that was spitting from the ECG machine.

"Haven't you guys seen a fella pass out before?" I joked, hoping to cover my embarrassment.

"Well, Dr. Sabine, you have had a cardiac event," the man reviewing the tape informed me. I didn't think I had had a heart attack. I was actually feeling fine.

"You had a cardiac pause," he continued. "Actually, two pauses."

"You mean my heart stopped?" I asked.

"Yes. The first pause lasted fourteen seconds," he said, looking at the readout. "Then, your heart beat once, and you had another pause eleven seconds long."

No one knew the cause, but I was going to be admitted until it was figured out.

My wife was apoplectic when I calmly called her from the ER on my cell phone to tell her where I was and what had happened. The news seemed so surreal to me.

Through the years, I have read a number of accounts of so-called "near death" experiences. I wasn't sure if my moment qualified, but I was surprised by how tranquil I was feeling. *If I were to have died, I would have died.* Matter-of-fact. No panic. Actually, I was experiencing a profound sense of peace. Everything would have been okay, whatever had happened.

Others who have been precipitously close to death commonly report seeing a light, often interpreted as a sign of the divine attending or inviting one at the point of departure. I was amused that instead of one light, I saw eight or ten lights racing past my vision in a counterclockwise direction, like racehorses blazing past me on the way to the post.

I was hustled up to a hospital room, hooked to an external heart monitor with a pacemaker function. Later that day, I was visited by my primary care physician, a general attending physician, and a cardiologist. They repeated my ECG and did an echocardiogram and a "bubble-test," a rather frightening procedure in which an air bubble is intentionally injected into a vein to see if there is a hole in the interior membrane of the heart. Sometimes, the procedure can cause a stroke if there is a hole in the heart and the bubble migrates through the hole and goes to the brain. Thankfully, in my case, I had neither a hole nor a stroke, only anxiety as I watched the monitor that tracked the bubble in its journey toward my heart like a life-or-death video game with a real life on the line. Fortunately, the bubble did not find a hole and stayed safely put.

When the tests were completed, I was given a diagnosis of "malignant vasovagal response," which meant my heart "rebooted" at unpredictable times. Under certain situations of stress or pain, or when my blood pressure might be out of control, my heart was inclined to pause longer than it should, causing lightheadedness or episodes of fainting.

My team of doctors recommended a pacemaker for me, which would adequately address the issue of inopportune fainting. We weighed the pros and cons of the device, but my tipping point in its favor was a hypothetical "you're driving along, and a truck is approaching from the opposite direction and your leg cramps..." scenario.

"Let's do it!" I said. I sure wanted to avoid the fiery crash.

The day after Thanksgiving, 1998, I had a brand-spanking new pacemaker installed. The procedure was completed without incident. A few hours in recovery, an overnight stay for observation, and I was sent back into my life with no more than a new bump protruding from the left side of my chest.

That night, disregarding medical advice to go home and rest, I took my wife Kay to the movies. I mean, what could happen in a movie, right?

We went to see "Meet the Parents," where Kay took the seat on my left. "Meet the Parents," starring Ben Stiller, is without doubt one of the funniest movies ever made. The comedy is driven by the creation of an empathy in the viewer based in the social discomfort of Stiller's character. Again and again, at a moment when a social interaction could not possibly get any more awkward, Stiller haplessly makes the situation worse.

When the penultimate moment came, Kay erupted in laughter with the rest of the audience. Impulsively, she swung her left hand across her body and smacked me right on my newly-installed pacemaker!

Her laughs immediately gave way to a gasp of horror as she realized what she had done. I sat there for a few moments, stunned myself by what had just happened, then burst into laughter at the look on her face. Not exactly what the doctor ordered, but I was relieved that I was still breathing and amazingly uninjured. Shaken, but otherwise alive and well, we went home and spent the remainder of the weekend adhering more closely to my recovery plan.

As the events of that remarkable weekend unfolded, there was a corresponding emotional struggle that was also developing. Up until that time, I had lived a charmed life when it came to my health. I have always been slender, perhaps in part because of the hyper-metabolism that goes with attention deficit hyperactivity disorder. I was sick with the flu or a virus only about once every three years. I ran three miles a day and perceived my body to be one of my assets. I was committed to good health. I was not expecting to see my health compromised until the distant future, when I had advanced into old age.

But here I was, forty years old and sporting a pacemaker. It didn't fit my image of myself. To make matters worse, a few months later I consulted a tertiary-care electrophysiologist of considerable reputation, who explained to me that he didn't think I had a malignant vasovagal response at all. He pointed out that I was on a tilt-table when I had my episode. When I was given nitroglycerin, my blood pressure began to fall, which was the objective at the time. Then, when the needle was jabbed into my wrist just after my anticipation of pain had been aroused by the nurse, I fainted, a classic vasovagal response. My heart had paused, as it does by design in these scenarios. It waited for me to fall prone, where it wouldn't have to work as hard to reboot.

My physiologist explained that because I was never prone, having passed out on the tilted table, my heart waited 14 seconds before it finally threw down a single beat. After eleven more seconds of waiting, my heart overrode the response and fell back into normal rhythm. The ER staff had inadvertently reproduced a series of actions that would induce anyone to pass out, he said. In fact, healthy people probably have cardiac pauses of similar duration all the time when in crisis situations, but they are not hooked up to monitors and nobody knows.

With his explanation of why my pacemaker was probably not necessary, I suggested that we schedule a date to get the hardware out of me.

"That's not a good idea," he said. "If we take it out, you would risk getting endocarditis, a potentially fatal heart infection."

"But doesn't my having a pacemaker essentially make me uninsurable, even if I don't need it?" I bemoaned.

"Yeah," he said. "Sorry."

"Great."

Resting that Sunday after my surgery, I was melancholic, a rare state for me. It seemed strange to see myself so differently. In the scheme of life, getting a pacemaker was not such a big deal. Having it didn't really affect my life expectancy. There were no restrictions on my activities, other than being prohibited from lifting heavy weight over my head, which could compress the leads of my pacemaker. My quality of life would really only be affected by the inconvenience of a twice-a-year checkup and the occasional playful head-butt from my three-year-old son.

The meaninglessness of all that had happened that weekend continued to weigh heavily on me as I got dressed for work Monday morning. *Why did this happen? I am forty years old, in great health, running three miles a day. I do everything I know to take care of myself. But, in spite of that effort, here I am with a new pacemaker. That's not the way things are supposed to work.* The pity party raged on as Kay put a new bandage over the incision, which was mostly hidden from view by my shirt collar.

I dragged out the door, feeling sorry for myself. First, I had to stop at the rehab hospital to see my patients there before I went to the office.

I went to Lorna's room to see her first.

"Good morning. How did your weekend go?" I asked.

"Not too well," she confessed. "I have no family here, so I sat around waiting for Monday to work on getting out of here. And I still can't get used to the idea of this pacemaker."

I smiled. "I know what you mean."

I pulled down the collar of my shirt so she could see my bandage.

Eyes wide, she asked, "What is that?"

"I got a pacemaker of my own over the weekend," I said.

"I am so sorry, Doc," Lorna said. With a wry smile, she added "I know you guys are supposed to have empathy for your patients, but I think you went a little too far."

"Nothing is too good for you, Lorna," I said, smiling too. I picked up the manual for her pacemaker from the top of her dresser.

"Let's see if we can figure these things out," I said, pulling a chair to her bedside. For the next few minutes we learned about the "newfangled gadgets" that had taken up residence in each of us.

Two days later, Wednesday, I sat down in my office with Daniel for his next session. Grief, as usual, stood between us. I enticed Daniel to play a game of checkers, but he sat through the game not looking at me, still mute. As we played, I noticed what a beautiful boy he was, and perhaps recognized a fraction of the pride his dead father must have felt. I searched in vain for a way to break open Daniel's sorrow so that he could emerge and meet me. I still didn't know much about him, but I wanted to.

Daniel had me on the ropes in the game. I sat looking at the board for quite a long time in silence, pondering my next move. As I did so, I sensed that Daniel was looking at me. I thought at first he was looking into my face, but I was not quite right.

Looking up at him, I said, "What is it, Daniel?"

"What is that?" he asked and pointed at my collar.

I suddenly realized that he was looking at the bandage peeking over my shirt collar. I was pleased that he had asked a question on his own and without my prompting.

"Well, that's kind of interesting," I replied. "Over the Thanksgiving weekend I got a pacemaker put in to help my heart. I know it sounds weird because I'm pretty young to get one."

"You are not so young to get one," he said with a faint smile.

At first, I thought he was making a joke about how old I was, although he had never joked about anything before. I thought maybe he was confused about what I had said.

"Do you know what a pacemaker is?" I asked.

"Yes, I do," he said. Then, he reached to his own collar and pulled it down to reveal a small telltale scar resting on top of a circular mound rising from his chest.

"My gosh!" I said. "You have one of your very own!"

Daniel sat quietly, his shirt collar tugged down. I sat there with mine pulled down, too. We were like two brothers of a secret society. From our outside appearance, we looked like everyone else, but just beneath the surface, with our pacemakers, we shared the same vulnerability and healing.

"Tell me about yours," I said simply.

"I got mine when I was just three years old," Daniel began. For the first time, he opened up to me, telling me his vague memory of getting the pacemaker implanted.

"What I remember most is that my dad carried me from the car when we got to the hospital. I rode in the back, and it was very early in the morning. When we got there my dad wrapped me up in a blanket. I was still in my pajamas."

Daniel sat for a minute with his eyes closed, quietly indulging the memory.

After a few seconds, I said, "Daniel, what are you thinking right now?"

"I can smell him. My dad. I can remember the smell of his aftershave when he was carrying me into the hospital."

A tear rolled down his face, his eyes still closed.

"Tell me what else comes to mind," I said.

For the rest of the session, Daniel told me about his father, speaking of him for the first time. His account was not the disconnected rehearsal of the past, so often heard when people tell their stories. It was an immediate, deeply felt testimony, allowing me entry into his relationship with his father. Somehow, the shared experience of a pacemaker had opened a door for us. Daniel had courageously invited me to enter into that story with him.

I felt as if I were actually present in his bedroom as Daniel recalled the ritual of bedtime he and his father had shared. I was in the stands at the baseball field watching a father swell with pride when Daniel rounded first base and the outfielder chased the ball to the fence. I was almost hearing the holy sounds of family as he recounted the laughter at the dinner table when his dad told his mom about the way Daniel had danced in an icy stream on a camping trip.

Over the remainder of our work together, Daniel remained connected to his father and to me. In every session, grief, deep and cold, flowed in the undercurrent, but at least it was moving. He never returned to the dark cocoon that had held his feelings hostage. He and I were free to cry, but we were also free to laugh as he shared stories of his all too brief passage with his father.

It occurred to me that although his father had been taken from him, Daniel had received a wonderful legacy in one short decade. Daniel knew what it was like to be precious in someone else's eye, to be loved without reservation or obligation, to be prized above all else.

When it comes down to it, that is the basic need we all have, to be loved unconditionally. If we can really have that experience, if we can actually know how much we matter, the question of our place in this world is answered once and for all. As much as we are heartbroken by the loss of a person who has loved us so deeply, we can still go on. We can survive. Our life will not be thwarted by that loss. Under the tender and watchful eye of a doting gardener, a child has taken root, and love runs leaf and vine through the whole wide world.

Just a few days earlier, I had been lying in my hospital bed, filled with self-pity. I had grown comfortable with a life of answered prayer, where things generally worked out and success and health appeared to be guaranteed. Now, all of a sudden, my body was carrying a tangible, circular, mechanical reminder of my own mortality. It felt like a timer of sorts, inexorably counting down the minutes till my death. Only forty-eight hours earlier, death had been an abstract concept.

But now, every time I took a shower, or gathered my son close to my heart, or laid my hand to pledge allegiance, I felt it. What was once distant, now seemed close. I no longer had the luxury of denial.

Why me? At the time, I had thought it was so unfair.

Now a week later, because of the encounters with a very elderly woman and a grieving young boy, my journey into self-absorption and self-pity came to an abrupt and merciful end. A pacemaker was, for me, a death-knock that had sounded, but only faintly. For Lorna, it was a steady homing beam, obdurately drawing her into the next life. For Daniel, the tender broken-hearted boy incarcerated by his grief, our pacemakers opened a door to his story. I could no longer argue that getting my pacemaker was a meaningless event.

Ten years have now passed. Very likely, Lorna is gone. If not, she would be over one-hundred-years old. Daniel is now about 20, a young man who lost his father half his lifetime ago. And I have passed 50. The average person gets about five to seven years out of the battery in a pacemaker. I am still tapping on my first one twelve years later. In the next few months, I will finally get the pacemaker removed so that a brand new one can be installed. I will still run a small risk of endocarditis, but I don't particularly worry about it.

At first, my pacemaker seemed to be a boulder in the middle of my life. Now it is just a small rock in the garden. It is still there, but it doesn't threaten anything's growth or survival. My little brush with death has, because of a couple of generous souls, become a gentle prodding to keep poking up through the soil and into life.

chapter four

ON THE RAZOR'S EDGE

*The edge of a razor is
difficult to pass over;
thus the wise say the road to
salvation is hard.*

—Katha-Upanishad

THE STORY to which I now turn comes from the bottom-dwelling memories of my youth. It has fermented in darkness for over two decades.

Murder and suicide are so grave and heavy, that as soon as they are dropped into the viscous pool of memory, they tend to sink from sight. I have left these memories undisturbed for a long time. I hope that all this time left alone has

*My dream, however
unlikely, is that the
alchemy of time has
worked a miracle.*

allowed some of the other ingredients of life to influence, or dilute, or perhaps even sweeten the essential bitterness of those tragic events. My dream, however unlikely, is that the alchemy of time has worked a miracle.

As Daryl pressed the barrel of the pistol against his temple, he felt a rising sense of anticipation. Not a bad place to kill yourself. No one around. The lake is peaceful. When they find me here, it will be a proper ending to this drama.

An hour earlier, he had waited for his wife, Robin, to arrive at her job at the grocery store. Getting out of her car, she was as beautiful as he had ever seen her.

"Robin," he called from his pick-up.

Robin wheeled around when she heard his voice. Daryl half expected her to run the other way. She had been warned by everyone to stay away from him. The consensus was that he was unstable. He might do anything.

But when she stopped and looked at Daryl, she ignored the advice and walked toward him anyway.

"What do you want?" she replied.

"Is that any way to greet your beloved ex?" he asked.

"I said, what do you want?"

"Robin, I just want to talk a minute about you and me and Connor."

"There is no you and me, and the judge will decide about Connor," she said.

Daryl leaned back into the truck and looked away. "You've got me all wrong. I just wanted to tell you about my plans. I'm moving out of town. You and Connor have suffered enough and the best thing I can do is get lost for a while. I just wanted to try to have a civil conversation with you before I go. We have history together and some of it was good."

"Lately, it's been hell," she said.

"You're right, and I don't want that for either of us anymore. I want to regain your trust. I'm not suggesting we get back together. I'm just saying we should at least be nice to each other."

"Where are you going?" she asked.

"Climb in for a minute. It seems weird to talk like this. Just sit here and listen, and then I'll get out of here."

Robin pulled the door handle and swung the door open, but paused.

"Come on," he said, "just for a minute."

She sat down in the truck, closed the door and turned to him.

"How's work going?" he asked.

"Work is fine, Daryl," she said. "But you are not here to talk about my work."

"I know," he said. "I just wanted to ask."

An uneasy silence settled between them.

Robin broke the silence first. She had some things to say.

"Daryl, I'm sorry I had to leave. And I'm sorry I had to take Connor away. I didn't mean to hurt you, but there was just no other way. You have been out of control."

Fingering the pistol concealed by his side, he said, "Well, I feel much more in control now. You have made me wish for death the past few weeks, both yours and mine."

Robin appeared unnerved by his words.

"What do you mean?"

"I've had a lot of time to think, and I have finally figured out how this all ends," he said.

Confused, she said, "There is a long way to go. We have a lot to figure out."

"It seems to me like the movie is over, and it's time for the credits to roll," Daryl replied.

With that, he raised the gun to her face so quickly that she didn't have time to react. She stared at the gun as tears began to roll down her face. She knew Daryl was perfectly capable of threats and games. He was a master of disguise who could flawlessly reflect any persona that the circumstance demanded. But she was the only one who knew the landscape of his ravaged mind. She was all too familiar with his ego, an insatiable black hole, and his narcissistic rages that had ultimately trampled their family to pieces. But this gun pointed at her face didn't have the greasy feel of manipulation. It was cold and abrasive. His countenance revealed a finality that made her panic.

Could this be the end of my life? What about Connor? I can't go now. This can't be happening!

Daryl felt a rush of power as he held the gun to her head. *Who holds the cards now?*

He strained to suppress a surge of compassion, random scenes of good times they had shared parading by in an instant. At first, this nostalgia moved him to reconsider his terrible plan, but the fury quickly returned as he recalled how he had seen everything he loved snatched away from him. She had taken everything, so why shouldn't he take everything from her?

It was easier than he had thought it would be. The simple flexion of a small muscle in his left index finger sent a single, unsparing bullet through Robin's head. Blood spattered on the passenger window, and her lifeless body slumped against the door.

Daryl felt a surge of adrenaline. His ears rang from the concussion of the pistol's report. He reached across Robin and opened the passenger door. With one push on her leg, her bloody corpse, a minute earlier the beautiful, lively mother of his only child, rolled clumsily to the ground.

Daryl threw the truck into gear and gunned the accelerator. The forward momentum swung the passenger door shut, and he roared out of the parking lot. In his rear-view mirror, he could see people running out of the grocery store in an attempt to help their co-worker.

Racing toward the lake, he felt the jitters that typically signal the lowering of an adrenaline-induced arousal. In its place, exhausted sobs rose. He was anxious for the final act that would release him from his pain. He had no idea what was on the other side of this moment. Whether it was the peace of mindless oblivion or the hell of a legion of demons awaiting his doomed soul, one way or the other, his course was now charted. There was no turning back.

He noted again the feel of steel against his head. Slowly and deeply, he drew a long, last breath. Then, with one more pull of his finger on the trigger, he plunged a three-year-old boy and two loving families into his hell forever.

Long before I became a psychologist, before I knew anything about the powerful internal tides and currents that sometimes propel someone onto the rocks of self-destruction, I met a young man named Daryl Dixon, only nineteen-years-old.

Daryl was one of a dozen children born to parents who owned a fruit stand in Henryetta, Oklahoma. Half of the children were right-handed, and half were left-handed. All twelve had blue eyes. Daryl was sandwiched between talented, bright siblings. He was the salutatorian of his high school class, but that made him an underachiever among the Dixon kids who, one after the other, claimed the valedictorian's spot at graduation.

I met Daryl on my very first day of college in the fall of 1976. I was stretched across the bed of my dorm room, talking to my tall, lanky roommate and best friend, Will. The door to our room was open, and without warning or announcement, in walked a handsome boy with a charming, crooked smile. He didn't say anything, just went straight to the full-length mirror on the closet door and started running a comb through his thick shock of sandy, reddish hair. He radiated energy in every direction. He attended to himself with what appeared to be great pleasure, and when he had arranged his hair just so, he pocketed the comb, paused for one last approving look, and then whirled around, looking at Will first, then at me.

"Hey boys, you are the newbies. I am sophomore extraordinaire, Daryl Dixon. And who might you be?"

Will and I looked at each other quizzically, then introduced ourselves.

"Welcome, boys, to Snowbarger Hall, and to the best time of your life. You are gonna love it here, and if you don't, you just give me a holler, and I'll straighten out your day pronto."

Turning to Will, he said, "Big man, what's your major?"

"Heck if I know," Will replied. "If I had to declare right this minute, I'd have to say I'm leaning toward majoring in cute girls from south of the Red River."

"Good choice," Daryl said, smiling his approval. "But I have found the Oklahoma gal my personal favorite as a subject of study."

Turning to me, he said, "And what about you, little man?"

"Religion," I said.

"Ah, a preacher boy! Excellent! Me, too. Are you liberal or a conservative in that religion of yours?"

"Conservative, I think," I replied.

"Good man," he affirmed.

I smiled broadly at his approval.

"Over there in the religion department, they got a couple of card-carryin' liberals. You gotta watch out for them."

"Thanks, I will," I said.

And without warning, he left as abruptly as he had arrived, leaving a warm aura in his wake. Will and I just sat there smiling at each other. At some level, we both believed we had just encountered one of Life's favored sons.

Over the next few weeks, Daryl and I found our way to one another and formed a friendship, the trajectory of which neither of us could have predicted. I was attracted to Daryl's charm, his confidence, and especially his way with girls, those heavenly creatures with whom I had precious little experience. Daryl seemed to be "on" at all times and in all situations. He was comfortable being goofy and playful, and he could snap the whip of his intellect on just about any subject whenever he desired.

Our common interests, dating back well before our first meeting, ensured that we would have ample opportunity to get to know each other. Both of us were religion majors and planned to enter the vocation of Christian ministry. We dreamed of being instruments of God to change the world and offer to people what we believed was the certain path to abundant life. We saw in each other the potential to be skillful ministers and we colluded in a secret and unspoken arrogance. Young men as gifted as we thought ourselves to be would someday be blessed with the pulpits of large, influential churches. Or perhaps one of us would head a wide-reaching para-church ministry that would bear our name. We thought it was only a matter of time before those dreams would be fulfilled.

We both joined the "Gospel Team," an itinerant Christian choir that travelled around the region on weekends holding "revival" services. Several young men on the team were allowed the opportunity to deliver the sermon at these services. In turn, both Daryl and I ascended to the pulpit and delivered the first sermons of what we knew would be long, celebrated, and blessed careers in ministry.

I look back now on our shared fantasies with embarrassment. Luckily, the arrogance of youth is shielded from insight by the sweetness and innocence from which it is borne. I must confess that those days, while fanciful, were heady and rapturous. To be young and enthusiastic and to believe that God's indelible seal of approval had been placed on you was powerful. Soon enough, experience, the unforgiving teacher, would reveal the futility of those once and future dreams. But for us, at that moment, all of the elements of a perfect saga were in place.

The arrogance of youth is shielded from insight by the sweetness and innocence from which it is borne.

As we grow older, we often look behind us with nostalgia and more than a little chagrin. Usually, the unfulfilled dreams are benign. The windmills of youth are precious to us because of their power to remind us that we are indeed "the stuff that dreams are made of."

Tragically, Daryl's story took an unexpected turn. Simmering just beneath the surface of

> *Usually, unfulfilled dreams are benign.*

Daryl's charm and boyish arrogance was a pathogen so virulent and fulminating that, once loosed, no one in his life would remain unaffected.

I passed the days of that long-ago freshman year in a rush of self-indulgence. Sleeping through church and class became routine as I availed myself of every opportunity to avoid responsibility. If you wanted someone to make a late night run to Taco Bueno, I was your man. If you asked me to cruise with you up and down 39th Expressway all night in the never-ending and never-fulfilled search for female companionship, I was ready. If you wanted to stay up and regale me with stories of your life, I was there, already the nascent therapist in the unlikely disguise of a bright-eyed freshman.

Sheltered and over-protected, I had little maturity to bring to the challenge of college life. One factor, "the calling," prevented me from completely failing in school and becoming another casualty of the lure of immediate gratification that derails so many college dreams.

Since seven years of age, I carried the belief that I had been tapped by God. While I lacked the discipline of behavior and character required for ministry, I had an unquenchable curiosity about life, and in the tradition in which I was raised, the only way to explore the question of life was to seek an encounter with the mystery of God.

For me, this was not an academic exercise. It was like grabbing hold of the lion's mane. You never knew what far away and exotic reaches you were going be flung to next, and you suspected you were going to be eaten before it was all over.

Though I was in no way immune to doubt, one consequence of that immersion into faith was that the divine seemed so imminent, so immediate, that at any moment, in class or late night discussion, the familiar aura might suddenly enfold me. Tears would begin to flow and my heart would begin to race. Breathtaking and humbling, life would break open and pull me in and say "yes" to me, as if I were the only beloved boy in the world.

I became a committed seeker of that enigmatic, transcendent experience of life and began to see it everywhere. As unlikely as it seems, theology and philosophy were unfailing in their ability to find a vein that ran straight to my heart and to make my head spin in mad visions. All I needed was someone with whom to share that bliss. Daryl was that someone.

In this pursuit, our paths were not entirely identical. Daryl's own interests led him into psychology and the bizarre world of quantum physics, while I tended to crave the ancient and modern philosophers, and especially the melancholic existentialists. But we were patient and committed teachers to one another. It seemed that when Daryl began to tell me about the amazing things he had read, he had infinite patience and would not let up until I saw it the way he did. When my mind was blown by Plato or Camus, I could not rest until I took Daryl through it, step by step. I should add that we seldom mastered any subject. Rather, we collected a few impressions, shared them with each other, and ran on to the next destination.

Only the narcissism of youth can weld souls together like that. We thought we were special and could only be understood and appreciated by those who knew the secret handshake, had been held in sway by the same forces, and had been wooed by the same cosmic lover. The connection we felt to one another sometimes surprised us both.

One day, I was walking across the mall of the college campus, in a particularly good mood, singing softly as I strolled along. Across the mall, I saw Daryl come out of the Student Union building, waving when he saw me. I noticed that his lips were moving as if he were talking to himself. As we drew near to each other, I could hear that he was not talking, he was singing. In amazement, we both stopped singing when we realized we had been independently singing the same song! Not only that, we were both at the same place in the song and singing in the same key! We didn't know whether to laugh or completely freak out over that bizarre coincidence.

So now you may understand how profoundly confusing, and ultimately heartbreaking, Daryl's ignoble murder/suicide was to me. I did not lose just my closest friend. I lost a safe mooring that had secured us both during our storm-tossed, tender years.

I thought we were made of the same stuff, Daryl and I. Yet I had no experience with the kind of hatred that had ultimately consumed my friend. Sure, I knew anger, and I had a special gift for pettiness. But his desire to have his ex-wife and mother of his only child *dead*? To take action that would deprive someone of life? Where the hell did that come from?

That question, more than anything else, is responsible for my sojourn into psychology. Daryl had reached out to me toward the end of his life. He had tried to use our relationship, cherished by us both for so long, to save him from himself. I had tried with all I had to pull him back from the precipice. But nothing I had done made any difference. In the end, the monster that had Daryl in its jagged teeth swallowed up our relationship and bent it to its own hideous will.

Throughout my career I have worked with homicidal and suicidal patients many times. Little by little, time and experiences with those patients have allowed me another narrative by which to understand Daryl's actions. Nothing I have discovered excuses his terrible choices. Some aspects of his thinking will remain inscrutable. But I know much more now than when I shouldered the coffin of my best friend on a cold February afternoon and carried it before his broken and bewildered mother and father and his eleven, sad, blue-eyed siblings.

Though I had no awareness of the clues to Daryl's critical vulnerability, they littered the path of our passage together. The first one came in the second week of my freshman year. One evening, Daryl and I were getting dressed for Gospel Team practice. As Daryl went through his primping ritual before the mirror, I noticed something strange.

"Daryl, why are you wearing three tee-shirts?" I asked.

Daryl laughed, "Because I'm too skinny, of course."

I sat on the bed looking over Daryl's shoulder and into the mirror. I tried to see his reflection like he did, but I could see no hint of anything "skinny."

"I don't get it," I confessed. "You aren't skinny at all. You're perfectly normal. Not skinny. Not fat."

"It's just one of those things. I am just more comfortable bulking up a little."

"But why?" I persisted.

Rather than be frustrated that I wouldn't let it go, Daryl paused, looking at his reflection with equanimity. "I suppose it goes back to when I was younger. I was a really skinny kid, and I was born eleven months before my mother had twins. It seemed everyone was always focusing on the twins and forgot about me. I remember only the attention I seemed to get at the dinner table. Imagine what dinner time was like with a mom and dad and twelve kids. You had to dive in or you might end up hungry. There were seldom any leftovers. As the meat passed by, Dad would say, 'You guys better eat up, or you'll end up skinny like Daryl.' And they would all stare at me like I was from outer space or something. I started wearing extra tee-shirts to look a little bigger and get them all off my back. I guess it still feels good, so I still like to wear them."

I accepted his explanation, even though it seemed odd. In hindsight, I think that story is emblematic of Daryl's struggle. In his family of extremely gifted, good looking kids, it was easy to drop out of sight.

Another clue came in Daryl's relentless quest to be accepted by women. He spent a great deal of time and energy talking to, hanging out with, dating, and generally winning over as many women as possible. While not exactly unique to Daryl, I see now how out of balance and compulsive that behavior was. But in my youth, Daryl's success with women was mythic and legendary. If I hadn't loved Daryl like my own brother, I would have surely burned with envy, like many other guys did. Instead, I determined to hang around with Daryl as much as possible in the hopes that a little feminine attention might come my way just by my lucky proximity to him.

One year, when the Sadie Hawkins Night rolled around and the girls on campus were deciding which of the boys they might ask out, Daryl and I were standing in line for dinner when a beautiful sophomore girl sauntered up.

"Hey, Daryl, I was wondering, if you don't already have a date for Friday night, would you go out with me for a pizza?" Her confidence was amazing to me.

Without thinking twice, Daryl answered, "I'll go with you, but only if you get a date for Dave."

I looked desperately for a place to hide, but alas, no such luck. Again, the girl's confidence was unshaken. "Done!" she said, "We'll pick you guys up at Snowbarger Hall at seven." And with that she wheeled her loveliness around and left as suddenly as she had come.

I stood there stunned by what had just happened. Daryl just clapped me on the back and said, "Way to go, man! You got a date!" Just like that, I had my first and last invitation to a Sadie Hawkins date. My humiliation over the fact that someone had to be coerced into arranging the evening was eclipsed only by the realization that I was going to have a date with, presumably, a real, live girl. *Man, that Daryl is awesome!*

In spite of my early admiration for Daryl's preternatural ability to impress women, I came to see problems. His needs were insatiable. Rather than settling into a committed, loving relationship, Daryl sought feminine approval from every quarter and at all times. It was not primarily a need for sexual conquest, although that was part of it. It appeared that he *had* to have the approval and admiration of every woman he met. He had a way of being flirtatious with women he found sexually attractive, but he was also able to lure, with a wink and a smile, women and girls from eight to eighty, into his charms.

He took great pleasure in the moment that a woman noticed and regarded him positively. What appeared as an adoration of women was actually a fierce dependency. They held the keys. If he was uniformly and universally loved by women, all was well. But if he was rejected or, even worse, if a woman was indifferent to him, he was deeply wounded. In those instances, he would attempt to win her over by any means possible. If she persisted in her indifference, he would be furious or lapse into depression for a time. When he was rebuffed, he resented and obsessed about that woman and her power over him.

Prior to meeting his wife, Robin, Daryl revealed his profound ambivalence about women and commitment. His girlfriend, Alice, was lithe and laconic, a docile, quiet, blonde-haired girl who seemed a fitting complement to Daryl's carnival antics. She smiled her approval when he was clever, and she blushed sweetly when he praised her in front of other people. From the beginning of their relationship, she, more than others, was able to bring Daryl a measure of peace and comfort in the midst of his otherwise manic life.

Daryl and Alice dated more than a year. She adored Daryl, and he began to ponder whether he might propose marriage. Besides being devoted, she possessed all the qualities of personality that he valued. But, although Alice was physically attractive, she lacked the classic idealized beauty that he always fantasized a wife of his would possess. I suspect he wanted his wife and him to make stunning first impressions when they entered a room. A "trophy wife" would be as fitting a description as any to describe Daryl's goal for a life-mate. Alice's understated beauty radiated without obtrusive show or pretense.

After a year, Alice began to worry about Daryl's lack of commitment. Daryl knew she would ultimately tire of his indecisiveness and move on, an outcome that scared him almost as much as marrying her. So, as a good religion major might do, Daryl decided to take it to God.

Ten minutes after the fact, he came shuffling into the dorm looking confused and disheartened. He looked like somebody had shot his dog.

"What's happened, man?" I asked. "What's got 'hold of you?"

"I've been talkin' to God about Alice," he said.

"Well, that's probably a good idea, I would think," I said.

"Yeah, you would think," he said. "I've been trying to figure out what to do about Alice. In Old Testament class, Professor Shelton was talking about how in the Bible, Gideon put out a fleece to determine God's will, right?"

"What does that have to do with Alice?" I asked, realizing as soon as I said it what was going on. "Daryl, don't tell me you put out a fleece about Alice."

"I did," he admitted. "I went to the prayer chapel and was praying for God to show me what I should do. You know, should I marry her or not."

As I looked at Daryl, despondent in the wake of his consult with God, I couldn't help wondering if he was sad because he was going to marry her or because he was not.

He continued with the events of his spiritual discussion. "I obviously couldn't come up on short notice with an actual fleece, so I decided I would flip a quarter. I prayed really hard, and asked God to just grant me this one request. If I flipped heads, He wanted me to marry Alice. If it came up tails, I should let her go."

"You flipped a coin to decide about Alice?" I asked.

"Yeah, I did. I was stuck, man. I didn't know what else to do."

I couldn't help thinking this was one of the dumbest ideas I had ever heard, but the suspense was too compelling to reflect. I wanted to hear what "God" had said with a quarter.

Daryl buried his face in his hands. "It came up heads," he said, peering at me through his fingers.

"Well, Daryl, is this your way of asking me to be your best man?" I quipped, not knowing what else to say.

"God, you're no help!" he said, throwing himself back onto the bed.

"Well, what do you want me to say? I guess this means you're gettin' married to Alice, right?"

Daryl let out a long sigh, followed by "not exactly."

I was confused. "I thought you said it came up heads."

Daryl looked up at me. "When it came up heads, I freaked out. So I went for two out of three."

This was vintage Daryl. He was so serious when he was telling me about this theological misadventure, but I found his whole story absolutely hilarious. Who else had the arrogance to try to force God Almighty into communicating through a coin toss, and then the audacity to second-guess the outcome? Only Daryl!

The constipated look on my face must have confused Daryl. He looked at me with his head cocked slightly, which tipped me into hysterical laughter. I had tried to hold back, knowing Daryl was struggling with a serious issue. When I looked up through my tears of hilarity and saw that Daryl was laughing too, I felt better.

Daryl told me the rest of the story of his encounter with God and the laws of probability. In the end, he had finally left the chapel after he had gotten to eight or more out of fifteen tosses.

After that, the relationship with Alice sort of petered out and they both went on to date and marry other people. I have often wondered what Alice thought when she heard the story of Daryl and Robin's tragic end. Whether or not God had a hand in what happened, I imagine she is, at the very least, thankful for Daryl's ambivalence.

Not long after their break up, Daryl cornered me in the Religion building coming out of my Church History class.

"Dave," he whispered, looking around in a manner both intense and conspiratorial. He pulled me out of the flow of our fellow students. "I think I have found her!"

"Found who?" I asked.

"I think I have found the one - my Dulcinea, my Beatrice! Her name is Robin. You have got to meet her."

I smiled at Daryl's exuberance, but Daryl found new "soul-mates" with astonishing regularity. Daryl was in love with being in love, and I suspected that he might never stay with one girl long enough to marry her.

I dismissed Daryl's raving and ranting about Robin that day as just another enthralling brush with enchantment. Time would reveal that Robin was not to be consigned to Daryl's repertoire of relationships come and gone. At the time, however, I never would have bet on it.

The following week, I looked up from my desk and saw a female, a petite brunette, standing at my door. Women were forbidden to be in the residential floors of our beloved Snowbarger Hall, a men's dorm. But there she stood, winsome and fine, light and lovely. Her green eyes seemed to reflect more wisdom than possible at her tender age. Slender but supple, she stood with one toe turned inward a bit, which only added to her doe-like appearance. She was as delicate a creature as I had ever seen.

"I am looking for David," she announced with a smile that caught me off guard. Although obviously impossible, I could have sworn her simple words were delivered with a hint of seductiveness.

"My name is David," I offered weakly.

"Hi David," she said in the same sultry tone, her smile broadening.

I was speechless. This was truly an unlikely, unprecedented occurrence in the life of a freshman religion major. In any room on each of the five floors of that cinderblock-and-steel dormitory, there has not, at some point, been a boy whose head hadn't reeled with the fantasy of just the sort of vision that stood before me now, in flesh and blood.

Had she designs on my skinny boyish form, I would have succumbed to chagrin on that very spot. Fortunately, I was spared such an untimely end when I heard the familiar music of Daryl's laughter rolling down the hall from just out of sight. I watched his two hands latch on to the vision's shoulders, and his crooked smile appeared beside hers as they watched me light up in a spectacular, crimson blush.

"Dave, this is Robin."

I managed to resolve my vapor lock. "Hi, Robin," I said, getting up to extend my hand.

Robin passed right by my hand and wrapped me in a warm hug. "I am sorry about that, David. Your buddy here put me up to that."

Releasing me, she sat down on the edge of my bed. "Daryl has told me all kinds of things about you. It is so nice to meet you in person."

I felt like a semi-celebrity. No one had ever talked about meeting me "in person" before. I liked Robin immediately. We closed the door, and she listened long into the night as Daryl and I performed the testosterone-driven dance of male bonding that inevitably occurs whenever young men are in the company of a beautiful girl. We told story after story that cast us as heroes, bold and daring. I had the sense that she delighted at being let in on the way Daryl and I regarded each other. She witnessed the tenderness and affection men sometimes share that is seldom revealed to women, and rarely admitted to one another.

Daryl and Robin did make a beautiful couple and were inseparable thereafter. Shortly after marrying my bride, Kay, I served as a groomsman in their wedding, and the four of us all became close friends.

Throughout our college years, Daryl and I seemed to relish the lives we were living, and it seemed our paths were in step. After graduating from college, we each went to seminary, although Daryl opted for Southwestern Baptist Seminary in Fort Worth, and I went to Nazarene Theological Seminary in Kansas City.

During his first year of seminary, Daryl went through a crisis of faith. Theologically, he had always been very conservative and believed in the literal interpretation of the Bible. I was more liberal and didn't have a problem viewing some scriptural passages as historical and others as metaphorical. This difference between us was the source of spirited debates. At first merely incidental, it would ultimately be an important factor in how each of us would negotiate our challenges to faith. Whenever I would encounter spiritual challenges, I was more intrigued, while Daryl was bothered. In one memorable college lecture,

Professor Ed Dexter came into our Systematic Theology class and posed the question, "Did the Virgin Birth really happen?"

We all looked at each other in consternation. Why would he ask such a question? The answer was obviously "yes." Professor Dexter smiled as a boy or two offered a hand and answered in the affirmative. When no one else wanted to weigh in, he raised his coffee cup and, to our dismay, pronounced, "Who cares?"

Professor Dexter was trying to make the point that faith is not based on certainty about the historicity of events recorded in scripture. In his view, it is instead about a personal relationship with God. This made sense to me, but not to Daryl. For him, all of it was true, or none of it was true.

When Daryl began to study biblical criticism in seminary, the wheels of his faith started squeaking and rattling. Despite his considerable intellect, his inflexible interpretation of faith dictated that there was no give and take in belief. Ultimately, the dissonance was not bearable, and he withdrew from seminary.

Over the next few months, Daryl struggled with his mission in life. Now that he was no longer going in the direction of a ministry, he was unsure about his future. I believed in him. If he would just commit, he would be successful at anything he attempted.

Daryl went to work for a company that sold programs to schools for their student fund-raising projects. Daryl was a natural salesman and excelled.

He and Robin welcomed a child, Connor, within months of the birth of our first child, Lauren. Kay and I went to visit Daryl and Robin when the babies were about one year of age. I was a still a seminary student, and we were barely eking by. On the other hand, Daryl and Robin were living in a new custom-built home in Oklahoma City, with a late model Porsche in the garage and two matching Cocker Spaniel's running around the house and yard. We sat the babies with the dogs on the floor and took photos. Daryl and Robin had quite an enviable life. We wouldn't have minded having those kinds of resources.

Within another year or two, Daryl left his sales job and started his own roofing company, quickly an entrepreneurial success. He seemed to have everything. He and Robin were in love, and Connor was growing more fine and bright with every passing day.

The tragic events that ensued seem impossible. Daryl was far from perfect, but he had a magnetic spark that made people love him.

But beneath the surface, his lifelong struggles with inferiority, which had driven and shaped him, still roiled and rumbled. His shining smile and confident manner thinly veiled his deep belief that he was defective—too skinny, smart but not smart enough, not worthy of attention and love.

His easy-going, carefree demeanor brought him a wealth of attention, but his ravenous ego was never sated. No matter how clever or funny or entertaining he might be, the tribute that was offered in return lacked any enduring substance, like cotton candy to a starving man.

Daryl kept his problems undetectable to others. But the powerful subterranean forces within were far from benign. The spark to light their fuse was about to be struck.

When Daryl had first started dating Robin, he confided that he and Robin had smoked marijuana a few times. This was not typical Nazarene "preacher boy" behavior, but neither was it alarming.

I had tried pot myself one weekend my freshman year when another freshman religion major offered me a taste of the forbidden weed. The experience was frighteningly pleasant. I could see how this could become a powerful temptation for me, and I never smoked pot with them again after that weekend. Seven more years went by before I even had my first taste of alcohol.

But when Daryl had told me he was taking prescription drugs recreationally, I was alarmed. He told me that Robin had a close friend who was a health professional and who regularly abused these drugs. This friend had a ready supply to share with Daryl. Daryl also told me he had bought a Physician's Desk Reference to research the drugs he was using. But rather than reading it to heed the warnings about abuse, he focused on how much he could take without reaching toxicity.

We were both steeped in a religious tradition that not only preached against drug use but deplored it as plainly sinful and a blatant rebellion against and subversion of God's preordained paths to joy. But for Daryl and me there were two paths that allowed us the convenience of a pass when it came to the church's rules.

First, we thought we were especially bright and that we could handle what derailed other people who were less gifted. We could calculate the risks to which others were oblivious and enjoy the experience without the negative consequences that entrapped lesser mortals. Second, we both felt constrained and deprived by the strict and inflexible rules maintained by the Church of the Nazarene, such as no movies, no dancing, or no co-ed swimming. Our lives were governed by a long list of "no's." We could live only so long under mandates that seemed so arbitrary before the little perpetrators in us jumped up and said, "I shouldn't have to suffer this way and be deprived of what are essentially rites of passage." For us, they were "rights" of passage that we were entitled to experience.

And so, what appears incongruent, that a Nazarene "preacher boy" would get mixed up in drugs, is actually not so surprising at all. What was surprising, however, was the tenacity of the drugs' grip on Daryl and how they immediately began to throttle him.

Daryl's experimentation with prescription drug abuse started in college. When he went to seminary, he had a job painting houses, where a regular part of the work day was sharing a joint with the crew before the first stop.

When he left seminary and his aspirations to the ministry, whatever was left of any inhibition based upon guilt evaporated. His curiosity was then tempered only by fear, and fear was systematically overcome as each new drug brought an exciting new high.

The reasons for the abuse of drugs are many. Some people, mired in depression or anxiety, use drugs to medicate themselves. In the ecstasy of the drug, they find a brief and welcome respite from the pain that causes them such suffering. Some are bored, finding themselves under the scourge of the mundane and needing a dependable path to excitement. Others find, in the fellowship of other users, a place to belong and a secret society that accepts them, if for no other reason than to worship at the altar of altered consciousness.

For Daryl, all of these motivations may have come into play at one time or another. But I think what drove him more than any other factor was his boundless curiosity. He delighted in exploring, absorbing, and understanding everything he encountered. Daryl and I shared this eagerness to know the world. Perhaps we were finally free of our sequestered childhoods and, like two puppies who found a breach in the fence, we couldn't stop putting our noses to everything we met. Everything had the exotic aroma of the new and unfamiliar.

When Daryl turned the spotlight on illicit drugs, he was entranced and trapped. In the wild, untamed, experience of being high, he found an ecstatic but illusory passage to his interior world, unlike any other he had ever encountered. In trying to describe it to me, he said it not only exceeded his normal experience, it did so by an order of magnitude that could only be conceived by insiders, those who had experienced it. It simply had no correlate in normal human experience.

Unlike the seemingly fickle and elusive God of his youth, who showed up on occasion and then went conspicuously absent at the most inconvenient times, this new deity was nothing if not dependable. Daryl had a fast-track to transcendence, and his new god never failed to deliver.

By the time Daryl realized that, rather than deity, he had made a deal with the Devil, he was too late. At our best, Daryl and I had explored the world in search of what was authentic and meaningful. We would not settle for the narrow, truncated world our parents inhabited. And the signal, the affirmation that we were on the right track, was the elusive but profound sense of ecstasy that from time to time marked the trail.

But the devil in the drug turned the tables on Daryl. Instead of ecstasy being the marker pointing to something else, it became the main event, the prize that was compulsively sought and which the drug consistently delivered, at least for a time. When the effects of the drugs began to wane, higher doses or new drugs would temporarily restore his bliss. And so, the path to ecstasy drew Daryl farther and farther from faith, family, and everything that had once been his.

Hope, the beautiful and tenacious sibling of Faith and Love, is always the last to remain in the house of our dreams. When the storm begins to pull our once proud and stable dwelling into the raging seas, Hope stays to

Hope, the beautiful and tenacious sibling of Faith and Love, is always the last to remain in the house of our dreams.

the last, even when the timbers are falling all about and the waters rush in. But once Hope is carried beneath the waves, all that once seemed so certain appears only as a fading and mocking memory.

I am not sure when Daryl came to the moment when hope was vanquished, but I know about when the descent began. In the spring of 1987, I noticed conspicuous periods of silence from Daryl. We always talked every few days on the phone, even when we could not see each other. I tried to call him, but Robin was evasive when she answered and I asked to speak to him.

Up to this point, Daryl had not told me how deeply he was involved with drugs. I knew something was wrong, so I told my wife that we were going to Oklahoma City to see Daryl for ourselves. On a Saturday morning, we showed up on Daryl and Robin's doorstep.

Robin's evasiveness was quickly surrendered when we were physically there before her. Without anger or anguish, she told us that Daryl had checked himself into a drug rehab. She was especially gentle with her words, as if she worried about what the news would do to me.

The next morning at visiting hours, I went straight down to the facility. Because visits were restricted to one person a day, Robin had given me permission to go in her place, feeling that my support might be helpful to him. I had never set foot in such a place. I didn't know what to expect, but I simply was not prepared.

I was led to the "day room," a dismal area with worn out and broken couches around a television set. Everything seemed a foot deep in the residue of a million cigarettes. There, in a tattered easy chair, sat my friend, showing no vestige of his former bright, cocky self. I felt a cold stab of fear as I noted his pallid complexion. He had aged a decade since I had last seen him.

While it was our custom to greet each other with a hug, Daryl sat there emotionless as I entered. He drew on the cigarette he held in his left hand and flicked the ash into a coffee can beside him. He blew the smoke up into the air, and then looked at me with a wan smile.

"Hey, buddy," he said.

"Hey, Daryl. How are you holding up?" I asked.

"Peachy," he said. "You?"

"I've been better," I replied. "I'm worried about a friend whose seems to be havin' a rough go of it lately."

"That sucks," he said, and twirled the tip of the cigarette on the edge of the can.

"I like the new digs, especially this designer wall paper," I said, relying on small talk.

"Yeah," he added, looking around, "and who knew couches came in this many plaids?"

As we talked, Daryl told me about how his life was falling apart. He pointed to the television set.

"A couple of nights ago, I was watching the news. I am just half payin' attention, when I see a reporter standing in my own front yard with this old lady who is one of my roofing customers. She is saying that she thinks I have left the country. She can't reach me and her roof is leaking. The reporter says they had also been unable to reach me. God, they think I am scamming people. It's toast, Dave. The business is gone. There is no way we can recover from that kind of bad press."

As he spoke, Daryl continued to fiddle with his cigarette. His blue eyes, formerly flashing, cutting, and sparkling, had been one his most striking features. As I observed my friend that day, those eyes no longer sparkled. The glorious blue was bleached out and pale.

But his eyes had not lost their ability to affect me. When Daryl told his story and he looked at me, his eyes were imploring and desperate. I decided at that moment, held in his disconsolate gaze, that I was going to save him. I would not let this happen to my friend, my companion through so many of the watershed moments of my halting and uneven youth. We had come a long way together. There was nothing that Daryl and I could not do if we put our minds to it.

In retrospect, I suppose that was my last moment of innocence. In the blissful and mythic dream of rescue, we would do battle with the dreaded dragon and win.

What we don't understand when we are young is that in real life, the dragon is not a stock plot device, setting up the inevitable victory lap for the conquering hero. The dragon is real. The fire burns. Sometimes, no matter how committed, the would-be hero is consumed. But that devastating lesson was further down the road. That morning, I accepted the invitation to battle. If Daryl was not able to hope for himself, I would hope for him.

"Daryl, tell me about this rehab thing. Give me the low-down on how this is supposed to work," I said, rolling up my sleeves.

Daryl told me about his program and mentioned that he was going off campus for a Narcotics Anonymous meeting in a few minutes. We asked the staff if I could go, and I was soon sitting in a circle with twenty addicts as they talked about "Step Two": *We came to believe that a Power greater than ourselves could restore us to sanity.* The "higher powers" around that table were a mess— vindictive, capricious, and unreliable. As a fledgling theologian and a budding co-dependent, I had to sit on my hands to keep from interrupting and setting them all straight.

Daryl and I bade one another good-bye that day with a belated hug. The last thing I noticed as I let go of him was that he still wore three tee-shirts.

I don't know how long Daryl maintained his sobriety upon discharge from treatment, but it was not long before he was full tilt again. His relapse scared Robin and she insisted that they separate until he cleaned up. She also forbade him to see his son, Connor.

Within a few weeks, I was awakened one morning at two a.m. by the phone ringing. It was Daryl.

"Dave, sorry to call so late. Can you talk a minute?"

"Of course," I said. "What is it?"

"This thing is killing me."

We had talked enough for me to know that he meant his addiction.

"Daryl, what is it? What has happened?" I asked.

"I'm tired," he replied. "Robin and I have been fighting again. We can't seem to deal with even the small stuff without fighting. And now I have these thoughts that run through my head. I can't stop thinking about this shit."

"What thoughts are you talking about?" I said.

"It's weird." His voice taking a distant tone, "I have these thoughts that I should kill myself. It seems so inviting. Not scary at all. I'm just tired of everything."

I sat up in my bed, now completely awake. Daryl's words chilled me, and I sat in stunned silence. Through the ensuing years, I have dealt many times with clients who are suicidal. It never fails to fill me with a sense of dread and sadness. Having been through the painful tutelage of my friendship with Daryl and its outcome, I know well the risks of suicide and the reality of the aftermath it brings. But at this time, in this phone call, I had no idea what lay ahead. I just knew I was entering a dark and unfamiliar land with precious little light of my own with which to navigate.

"Where are you right now?" I asked.

"I'm at a pay phone at Love's Country Store in OKC."

"Daryl, buddy." I said, trying to pull him back to me over the distance. "This is nuts. You are NOT going to kill yourself. There is an answer here. I know it's tough, but you are not thinking straight."

"That's not all, Dave," his voice lowering. "One of the thoughts I keep having is that I should kill Robin too. I've been carrying my gun around in my truck all day and I can't stop these thoughts."

As Daryl delivered that brief sentence, the words just hung there, unadorned and pendulous. I felt the darkness deepen. Desperation and panic welled up in me. I knew Daryl had a flair for the dramatic, but his words carried no hint of the theatrical this time. At any other time in our lives, I would have dismissed such words out of hand. But impossibly, here we were. My mind raced. In an instant my heart poured out a prayer for wisdom. My fantasy of rescuing Daryl from drug use was overwhelmed by this far more urgent and monstrous threat.

"My God, Daryl!" The words burst from me. "Listen to yourself. This is way out of hand. You have got to get out of there. And I mean tonight. You get in that truck and drive home. If our friendship means anything to you, you have got to do this. I have never asked anything of you like this before. But get out of there now. Will you promise me that you will go right now?"

His long pause stopped my heart. "Okay," he finally said.

"What did you say?" I asked, hoping I heard what I thought I heard.

"I said okay, Dave. I'm going. I'll go right now. You are right."

"You swear!" I couldn't feel assured.

"I said okay! I swear!"

"All right. You have four hours to get home, and you call me back. I am not going anywhere until you call, do you understand?"

"Sure, buddy. I'll call you," he said. "And, Dave?"

"Yeah?"

"Thanks, man."

"Don't thank me, Daryl. Just call me when you are home and safe."

"Right."

I hung up knowing I was done with sleep for the night. In 1987, before cell phones, all I could do was wait. As the sun was coming up that morning, the phone rang, much to my relief. Daryl told me he had given the gun to his folks and had actually checked himself into a psychiatric hospital.

Over the next two days, I relaxed a little, knowing Daryl was getting help. But over the previous few months, Daryl had been in outpatient psychotherapy and was savvy to the way the system worked. He knew that if he checked himself into the hospital, he could check himself out in 48 hours, and that was precisely what he did.

He later told me he had talked at considerable length with his psychiatrist about his fantasy of killing Robin and himself. He said his doctor, in a rather unorthodox response to this threat, remarked that if Daryl acted on that terrible fantasy, he would personally go to Daryl's grave and piss on it. I wondered if the therapist had said this to play on Daryl's sense of control, hoping that it would register with Daryl that death was the ultimate loss of control. Then again, maybe the doctor was just getting ticked off at Daryl for wasting time on such a senseless notion.

When Daryl called just two days later, out of the hospital but still very depressed, I invited him to come to stay with Kay and me for a while, until he felt better. Daryl accepted our invitation and later that day, he rolled up in our driveway in the inner city of Fort Worth, Texas, where I served as a pastor.

We gave Daryl my daughter's room to sleep in for the time being. Over the next few weeks, Daryl stayed with us and ate dinner at our table. I moonlighted as a roofer to supplement the seventy-five dollars a week that I received in salary from Liberation Community. Daryl worked side-by-side with me.

I was encouraged that Daryl seemed clean since coming to Fort Worth, and I hoped the cycle of addiction had been broken. In spite of the progress he had made in sobriety, though, he was far from okay. Daryl was suffering from Major Depression, but all I knew at that time was that my friend had changed. I could not reach him. We would sit up and talk late at night, but we weren't connecting. Our love for each other was still there. The mutual respect was as evident as ever. I was frightened to see the friend who I knew so well, right there in front of me, was unreachable.

One night, Daryl and I watched a feature film, *The Razor's Edge,* starring Bill Murray and based on a book by the same title by W. Somerset Maugham. The epigraph in the book was taken from the Katha-Upanishad. "*The edge of a razor is difficult to pass over; thus the wise say the road to salvation is hard.*" The movie's hero, Larry, is a pilot who is shaken by his experience in war. He rejects all of the traditional, but inadequate, paths that tempt him, paths such as material wealth, social status, even romantic love. He seeks transcendent meaning, something that stands above both the noise and the paths that are well-travelled but colorless.

When the movie was over, Daryl lit a cigarette and leaned back in his chair, deep in thought.

"Wow, that was awesome!" I said. "What a great film."

"You think so?" Daryl said dispassionately.

"Absolutely," I responded. "I thought it was both moving and inspiring. You know, authentic existence and the effort required to resist the call to compromise are all worth it in the end, however difficult the path to get there."

"I don't know," Daryl said. "Honestly, it's a nice story, but I'm not sure about the narrow path to salvation and all that crap."

"Crap?" I said, getting a bit worked up. "You are talking about a narrow path, but to those who have reported back—you know like Jesus and the Buddha and Thoreau and Gandhi—it sure sounds worth it."

"I'm not so sure. Maybe it's more of a karma thing. You get back what you put in. And I musta' put in some pretty bad stuff back down the line, 'cause from where I sit, this ain't gonna turn out good," he said in his best Eastern Oklahoma dialect.

I was confused. "The Razor's Edge" was just the sort of story about challenge that in earlier times would have deeply moved Daryl. But as he sat and smoked, his every pore seemed to signal resignation and giving up. Whatever tack I took, ennui met me. I just could not get through to him.

Whenever I push myself to recall the events of the weeks that followed, I quickly begin to sense the return of my old but formidable acquaintance—

my shame. I should have seen it. Although I had no training at that time in psychology, and I knew nothing about suicidal or homicidal thoughts or the accompanying risks, I should have seen it. The time has come to tell on myself.

The first ominous sign from Daryl came when he started talking again and again about a song by Oran Juice Jones called *Walkin' in the Rain*. I have not listened to that song in all these years, but as I was writing this, I looked up the lyrics and watched the video on YouTube. The song is about a man who follows his lover and sees her walking and holding hands with a man he presumes to be her lover. He is crushed by this betrayal and goes back to their home. He cancels all of her credit cards, throws out all of her clothes, and sells all of her jewelry. When she returns home, he chides her and throws her out. In the end, the woman, formerly beautiful and stylish, is seen with filthy, unkempt hair, standing under a bridge in an old white tee-shirt.

Late in the song comes the lyric that Daryl latched on to, that nauseate me still.

> *I'm so upset with you I don't know what to do*
> *You know my first impulse was to run up on you*
> *And do a Rambo.*
> *I was about to jam you and flat blast both of you.*

A "Rambo" referred to Sylvester Stallone's character, a killing machine, in movies by that name. In each movie, Rambo leaves an unbelievable trail of death in his wake on his way to righteous vengeance. When Daryl talked about his obsession with this song, I was bewildered. I had never known Daryl to act in violence toward anyone. In fact, he would retreat from those rare situations he couldn't talk his way out of.

As we roofed side by side through that hot summer, Daryl told me that the song literally ran through his head for hours at a time, and he just couldn't shake it. I asked him if Robin was seeing anyone else, and he said he didn't think so, but the idea of it drove him crazy.

The next clue I should have heeded was that Daryl was obsessing about weapons. He told me he found himself again and again driving past pawn shops, fantasizing about going in to buy a gun.

"Daryl, why in the world would you do that? I asked.

"Dave, I just can't help it. The draw is so powerful. Some days I resist, but then on another day I will give in."

The last clue came when Daryl showed up at our house with a brand new color television.

"Hey, what's this?" I asked.

"It's a gift," he said. "You and Kay have been so good to let me stay here without paying any rent. I just wanted to do something nice for you. It's no big deal."

I knew Daryl was in financial trouble. Legal fees and the failure of his business had led to a huge debt load. I knew what he had been earning when he was working with me, and it was not enough to allow him to buy this TV. But I took it anyway.

"Thanks, man. That is awesome!" I said.

With that, he walked around to the back of his truck and lifted out his golf clubs.

"Dave, you play golf with that crappy set that's not even complete. I have tried this game. You love it, but it's not for me. I want you to take these and enjoy them."

"Thanks, Daryl," I said, incredibly pleased.

I stood there with my friend in the driveway, leaning on my new clubs.

"Dave, I am going to go to Austin for a few days," Daryl informed me. "I met a new girl, and we are going to hang out down there for a while."

This didn't surprise me at all. Although Daryl had been through a lot of losses, he had never lost his ability to charm the girls. I thought maybe a few days away would help him turn the corner, get his mind off of Robin, and quiet the tapes that played relentlessly in his head.

We talked a few minutes, and Daryl said, "Well, Dave. I guess I better get going." He climbed into his truck and rolled down the window.

"Drive safe, Daryl," I said. "Have a good trip."

Daryl sat for a second, smiling. "You are a good man, Dave. Take care."

He waited just a few more seconds, then rolled up his window, lit a cigarette, and smiled that crooked smile before he nodded and pulled away.

The important moments of life are often attended by pomp and fanfare. Graduations, weddings and confirmations are celebrated with all manner of tribute and recognition. But at other times, the watershed moments come unannounced and pass by without hinting at their gravity. On that autumn evening, as I watched my closest friend drive away, I did not know that our time together was over, that I had seen that dazzling, crooked smile for the last time.

As his last days approached, Daryl, perhaps in preparation for what was to come, had taken an interest in reincarnation. He read Shirley McClain's controversial book *Out on a Limb*. I don't think he could approach his death without trying to make it an experiment or an adventure of some kind. He told me that if he ever decided to kill himself he was going to record the whole thing and leave it for me so that I might be able to learn from his experience, if there was anything to learn. He said that if he went before me, he would send me a sign in whatever way he could.

All of that sounds so morbid on this side of those long ago events. But Daryl was always pushing the envelope and speculating about what was out there on the margins of life. And so, incredibly, I thought nothing of it.

A few days later, Bryan Stone, my partner in ministry at Liberation Community, rolled into the same driveway from which I had said goodbye to Daryl. Bryan walked up to me with his head down, and I knew something was wrong.

"Dave," he said hesitatingly.

"Yeah, hey, Bryan," I said. "What's up?"

"Have you heard about Daryl?" he asked.

I knew in an instant that Daryl was gone. It also registered with me immediately that I had had no hint, no premonition.

"What happened?" I asked.

"He shot himself by Lake Overholser," he said.

"What?" I asked. "I thought he was in Austin. What was he doing in Oklahoma?"

And before Bryan could answer, I fell back, staggered by the sudden realization of what had happened.

"Oh God! Robin!"

Tears welled in my eyes, but just before that shock set in, I heard Bryan say, "She's gone too, Dave. He shot her in the parking lot of the grocery store."

The next few days remain a blur. I was pallbearer for my friend as he was laid to rest in his hometown. I did not feel the rage that day. That would come later, rage at Daryl for what he had done to Robin and his son, Connor, and to both of their families, and to himself, and to me, and to everyone else who had loved him. I was, for that day, a grieving friend who recalled him as a bright nineteen-year-old boy smiling at my mirror in the dorm as he combed back his hair. I saw him standing in the pulpit, preaching his heart out to a crowd of people nodding approvingly. I felt his love for me, remembering our talks about the successful lives boys like us were destined to lead.

Now, over twenty years later, I understand much more about the narcissism with which Daryl defended himself. I realize now how that cockiness was just a thin veil hiding a deeply insecure, lost little boy whose siblings weren't able to remember anything notable about his childhood at his funeral. He was the boy who wore three tee-shirts all his life, chased by the shame of perceived inadequacy. He bet it all on a long shot—that out there somewhere was enough attention, approval, and acceptance to make him whole.

From a clinical standpoint, I can explain how Daryl's once bright light went out, extinguished by a series of catastrophic failures; and how his rage over feeling victimized, no matter if distorted or mistaken, led him to take up the gun of the perpetrator.

Whenever there is a tragic, senseless loss, those who survive comb through the wreckage looking for answers. We want to know why. Somehow, knowing more makes us think we will feel better. And when we don't feel better, we resort to blaming ourselves. I have done a lot of that over these years. Why didn't I have the wherewithal to see the signs that should have been so obvious? Why had I colluded with Daryl in narcissism and superiority? Surely, there were many other things I could have done that might have changed the outcome.

I have done a lot of questioning and self-examination. But I have now come to realize that I can't condemn myself forever for what I did or didn't do. Daryl murdered his bride, Robin, and turned the gun on himself. That is the sum of it.

His life ended there. Mine has gone on. I, too, have had to face the demons of both arrogance and shame, and I have hurt those I love in innumerable ways. Though not immune from self-destructive choices, I have never been inclined toward suicide. In part, because of Daryl's tragic example, I have decided to live.

Coda

On a sultry summer day in June of 2010, I made my way back to Henryetta, Oklahoma. I had not been there since the day we buried Daryl twenty-three years earlier. His parents, now in their 80's, and several of his siblings still live in the area. By making the trip, I had two hopes.

First, I wanted to share the chapter about Daryl with his family in hopes that, even though I knew it would dredge up pain, it might also open a window of long-needed insight into why he chose such a path.

In typical Dixon fashion, they impressed me from the start with their intelligence and inquisitiveness. Within a few minutes of sitting down together, the awkwardness of the meeting was overcome. The air seemed thick with emotion. We cried and laughed together as we once again huddled around the memory of their bright and talented boy. His mother, the amazing force of nature who had raised twelve kids and has had to say goodbye to three of them, looked right through me with steel-blue eyes, ever-vigilant, searching still for the comfort that has eluded her. We went to the cemetery together, and as I stood at the grave of my friend, she paced around, never staying put for long, as if the only way to bear her loss was to keep moving, lest the full weight of grief settle upon her after all of these years.

The second hope was selfish. I wanted to heal myself. I have been haunted by my friend because I, too, have contended with the seductive face of narcissism with all of its hidden insecurities. I, too, have maintained an impressive collection of masks and have worn them to take from others what I thought I had to have. I, too, have failed myself and the family that has loved me. After thirty years, my marriage came to an end. My parents, like Daryl's, wonder what happened to their boy. Like Daryl, I am confronted by the loss of everything that I thought would be necessary to be happy.

And so, I opened up this old wound and looked for help again, as I have so many times from my friend, long-gone but still somehow never far away. As I read aloud the final two pages about our last few days together to Daryl's family, I broke down in tears. I recalled bitterly how I had failed to help Daryl see past the terrible choices he was contemplating.

What Daryl's family could not fully understand was that I was not only grieving for Daryl, I was grieving for myself also. But where Daryl was unable to see the good in himself, I am determined to find it in me.

As the life I have built over fifty years slips beneath the waves, scuttled sometimes by my own weaknesses and failings, I am in search of a safe and sheltered cove, a place where I can build a new vessel, this time made of materials that will last.

Daryl, I wish you could have been here, buddy. I wish you had come with me. I wish you had been a witness to all the moments of my life—both proud successes and frustrating failures. It would have been so much better to have you along.

I wish you had known the joy of Connor's first day in school, his first base hit, and an infinite series of moments you missed as he grew. Connor would have been so much better off to have known you, and to have the chance to embrace his dad, and to realize that you are a vital part of him. I don't think he knows you ever existed, and that breaks my heart.

I wish you could have had the painful but powerful experience of seeing Robin move on, and then coming to realize you were still standing, and that the only thing that can finally thwart the loving hand of Life is your own freedom to dismiss it. I so wish you had not dismissed it. You missed out on a lot, my friend.

Daryl, beneath all of the fervent debates that we used to have in our youth was a question so basic and so foundational that we never asked it out loud. But I see now that it was the question whose answer we sought so passionately back then. With our lives, we have written, upon our own page of history, what we believe the final answer to be.

The question reads something like this: "Is the last word on being human a 'yes' or a 'no'? When it is all said and done, when life is driven down to its lowest common denominator, is the final sum positive or negative? Do death and pain and loneliness and despair sound the last note? Or does the sweet harmony of hope and love and faith and home and friendship finally ring loud and clear above the fray?"

"Is the last word on being human a 'yes' or a 'no'?

It is clear to me that you believed the answer to be "no." Your actions and your choices recorded your answer. And you wrote the answer in anger and in blood.

I have now lived for half a century, and honestly, I can see that my life has been ambiguous in the way it records that answer. Sometimes, I have championed Life and all of the beauty it reveals. Many who know me would probably say the balance is in the positive. But few know just how often I have forsaken Life, how I have scrawled all over that beauty in the ugly graffiti of pettiness and dishonesty and selfishness.

But, Daryl, as I stood at your grave last week, and I saw your name and the dates of your lifespan, I wanted to go back and have the old argument again, to try and reach you and prevent you this time from coming to your devastating conclusion.

I know I can't do that. Life just doesn't appear to go backward. But I did come to another realization as I stood there. I realized that, in this great debate, you gave me the last word! You might have made your closing argument first, but I have yet to complete mine. I still have time.

The way I finish this life will speak my answer to all those who follow. And so, when I am laid to rest, and I am relegated with you to the past, I want my kids to place a simple headstone on my grave. I want, like yours, for it to record my name and my dates of birth and death. And I want them to add one more word, this one in bold capital letters. I want that last word to be "YES!"

chapter five

THE WOMAN IN THE YELLOW MASK

> *"Man is least himself when he talks in his own person. Give him a mask, and he will tell you the truth."*
> —OSCAR WILDE

AGNES CAME INTO our first session with a scowl on her face. From her countenance and gait, she appeared like a woman inching her way down a dark alley. Her eyes darted back and forth, but never strayed from me for very long. When she launched herself onto the couch in my office, I could tell an interesting session would follow.

She didn't say a word, but began rummaging around in her cavernous purse. I was afraid to speculate as to what she was looking for. She produced a number of odd items and piled them beside her: a roll of masking tape; a light blue, chandelier-shaped beaded earring; and a collection of magazine clippings that had been folded and refolded. She continued to look deeper until she finally excavated the prize she had been looking for—a yellow mask.

I was curious about the significance of the mask. Had she worn it to some important affair? Was it a trinket from childhood? What did it mean? Unfortunately, she gave no answer as she quietly lifted it to her face and fit the elastic band around her head. She then stiffened her back and raised her head, defiantly challenging me to proceed with therapy.

Agnes was a 40-year-old Caucasian woman whose outstanding quality was her, well, her remarkable homeliness. Skin of unhealthy pallor was too

The dedicated therapist always looks for something in the patient to value and respect.

abundant for her skinny frame. Faded green eyes protruded from their dark sockets in an unblinking stare that half spoke fear and rage. An aggressive acne had pitted her face. Thin lips and yellowed teeth formed an angry snarl. Cheekbones succumbed to prominent jowls, and came together in a sharply receding chin. A failed attempt at pulling back her strands of oily, thinning brownish hair left her incessantly brushing it away from her face.

The dedicated therapist always looks for something in the patient to value and respect. As I searched for such a quality in Agnes, an ancient passage came to mind.

He had no beauty or majesty to attract us to him,
Nothing in his appearance that we should desire him.
He was despised and rejected by men, a man of sorrows,
And familiar with suffering.
Like one from whom men hide their faces he was despised,
And we esteemed him not
(Isaiah 53:2-3, Holy Bible, NIV).

In our first session, I sat in the wing chair, which has come to be known as "my chair." Over time, I have noticed that where on the couch opposite my chair a patient sits is telling. The ones who opt to sit on the near end of the couch across from me in the first session are more likely to tend toward emotional enmeshment and diffuse personal boundaries. For others, the place at the far end of the couch is preferred. Often, these patients are less comfortable with intimacy and are much more cautious.

Almost no one sits in the middle. Except Agnes. She sat squarely in the middle of the couch and glared.

I began the session with my usual opening, "What brings us together?"

Agnes sprang to the edge of her seat and was almost shouting. "Oh, come on!" she screeched and glared all the more.

Taken aback, I said, "Agnes, I don't know what you mean."

She held her rigid posture, defiantly staring, apparently implying that we both knew why she had come and that I was being impossibly transparent in trying to get her to play the "therapy game"—as if I didn't know.

"Truly, I don't know the reason you have come to see me," I said.

With a sigh of contempt, she rolled her eyes dramatically. She took a deep breath, held it for a moment, and then unloaded.

"Come on, man. You're a crazy man! Can't you see I've gone nuts? At least that's what my stupid parents think. They made me come," she said too loudly for the circumstance. I worried the people in the waiting room might hear and wonder about the commotion.

"I'm goin' round the bend," she ranted, ripping the mask off of her face, "and when they die, I'm gonna end up on the street eating biscuits out of the garbage, man. What do you think of that? I'm forty years old, man, and nobody loves me except for my stupid parents and they only do because they have to."

Then even louder and faster, she seethed, "My life is empty, man. And there's not a thing you or anybody else can do about it. Hell, you won't do anything about it, because none of you give a damn about me!"

On and on, she spat out her litany of grief. She reeled off ten issues in less than a minute, and I sat dumbfounded, not knowing how to begin. Finally, I inserted a compliment into one of the rare pauses in her tirade. I said, "Agnes, I really do think you are a valuable person."

Wow, Doc, I thought. *Is that all you got? How lame is that?*

Apparently, Agnes was even less impressed with my contribution to the discussion. She sat incredulous that I had the audacity to utter such a bald-faced lie.

After my ensuing uneasy silence, she leapt up from the couch and charged toward me. Caught off guard, I didn't react when she rushed me. Her charge halted suddenly, with her nose about two inches from my nose, her pale eyes staring through me, "eyeball to eyeball," as we say in Texas.

"Just look at me, man! I'm ugly! You look me in the eye and tell me I'm not!" she shouted.

Sadly, I agreed with Agnes's self-assessment. I had judged her to be ugly, and she knew it. All I could say was, "Agnes, why do you ask me such a question?"

Agnes blinked and sat back down. She gave no hint of awareness that she had accosted me only moments before.

"You know, my daddy worked for the FBI, and he is a genius." With that she was off and running on another random tangent.

Countless assumptions are made that beautiful people are talented and capable long before they are experienced as such, and someone unattractive is viewed as average at best, and rejected out of hand at worst.

Although relieved, I knew I had failed in my mission to find a quality I could love in her. And she had called me on it.

The truth is, Agnes spoke my fears as well as hers. The hazing I had endured in childhood, my fears back then of never marrying still reverberated in me. I recalled watching Bill Gann, the consensus hunk in my high school, swagger to the girls' delight after another inspired performance on the football field. I stood by, apparently invisible, wondering what his life must be like.

We never admit publicly that a particular person is ugly, but we often prejudge the "ugly" population very negatively. Countless assumptions are made that beautiful people are talented and capable long before they are experienced as such, and someone unattractive is viewed as average at best, and rejected out of hand at worst.

I had hopefully come to terms with my own insecurities about physical appearance. Losing one's hair around seventh grade tends to accelerate this adjustment. However, memories of being marginalized and alienated still haunted me. A lingering maxim still had power: "When you are the second biggest geek in the class, keep your distance from the biggest geek." Being too close to their unattractiveness might mean you became collateral damage, as surplus derision and rejection landed on you, too. Therefore, compassion for

Agnes posed a challenge for me. I didn't want to stand too close.

After limping through our first session, I tried to analyze the significance of Agnes's accessories. The yellow mask, I thought, was an expression of her embarrassment, and she was perhaps even attempting to spare me the pain of looking on her unseemliness. But other odd tricks soon appeared in her repertoire.

Our second session began with Agnes walking through the door already spewing. "What's wrong with your dang secretary? She keeps lookin' at me. Hasn't she seen crazy before? She works in a shrink's office, for God's sake."

"Agnes, please come in. Sit down here and tell me what happened," I said.

"What do you care, baldy?" she yelled. As soon as she said this, she appeared mortified by her retort. With wide eyes, she snapped out of her rigid pose and dove into her purse, throwing things out until she seized upon a roll of masking tape. She tore a piece off and proceeded to tape her own mouth shut. She then sat back and stared at me, mute but seemingly satisfied with her problem-solving strategy.

Finding an appropriate diagnosis for Agnes was difficult. My first impression was that Agnes was schizophrenic. She was tangential in her thought, bizarre in her dress and behavior, and paranoid, accusing me of secretly planning to bill her poor parents and leave them destitute. What didn't fit the Schizophrenia hypothesis was her lack of visual or auditory hallucinations. Also, she wasn't apathetic. Instead, she had a powerfully *negative* affect. She was livid and angry at the world.

Agnes mysteriously alluded to a dreadful event when she was fourteen, but weeping bitterly, said it was too painful to talk about. Had she been raped? Had someone molested her when she was a child? Had she witnessed some great trauma? Perhaps Post-Traumatic Stress Disorder was the proper diagnosis.

Dissociative Identity Disorder, also known as Multiple Personality Disorder, was a possibility. Perhaps she had experienced some abuse so great that she had split off parts of herself to survive.

Over time, Agnes and I engaged in a sort of therapy version of a game of cat-and-mouse over the issue of what had happened to her. I was definitely the mouse. But as labile and extreme as her affect was, she always presented the same essential personality.

Another plausible hypothesis was a personality disorder. Agnes was certainly histrionic. Perhaps she had Histrionic Personality Disorder. She compulsively sought my affection by being overly dramatic and seductive. Borderline Personality Disorder was a possibility. The borderline personality is characterized by a number of the qualities Agnes possessed. She was terrified of abandonment, and all her relationships were volatile. She would speak of her poor mother with great sympathy one minute, but in the next, her mother was vilified for making her life a living hell. She was impulsive and prone to spectacular fits of anger. She often spoke of her feelings of emptiness.

Many therapists have noted a phenomenon regarding diagnosis of their patients. Psychiatrist Irvin Yalom has articulated the forces of the phenomenon particularly well. One would think that the more times a therapist sees a particular patient and the more information is gathered about that patient's life, the easier it is to arrive at the right diagnosis. Yalom notes, however, that the converse is often observed. Diagnoses are driven by lists of criteria and designed to lump people into categories. The more experience a psychotherapist has with a patient, the more the patient becomes a rich, three-dimensional, complex individual. Consequently, the diagnostic categories the therapist was confident of just a few sessions ago now fail to do justice to the person and the complexity of the presenting problems.

Agnes presented another difficulty. She behaved in ways that revealed important diagnostic information, but she was an unreliable historian. Sometimes she remained tightly guarded about issues whereas other times she reported false information altogether.

Guardedness is one form of "resistance." I was taught to honor the patient's resistance. When the relationship is safe enough, the patient will step forward and deal with her painful experiences more fully. So, I waited. I would gently open the issue, and when Agnes firmly slammed the door on my fingers, I would pull back and wait again. And wait. And wait. For one year I waited, and I still knew no more about what had happened when she was fourteen.

She grieved deeply, almost desperately, that she had been a disappointment to her parents. She spoke about having been a beautiful little blond 5-year-old girl, and how high her parents' hopes had been. Now, she said, they were saddled with a crazy child when they should have been happily enjoying grandchildren. On the days when this grief arose, her parents were like tragic heroes, gambling their love and life on the joy of a child, only to have that child become a monster who needlessly and endlessly eroded their dreams. In spite of Agnes's halting, tangential manner of speaking, the cadence and tenor of her grief were strangely poetic.

Her anger was another story. On certain days and for no apparent reason, Agnes whirled into the office leaving destruction and confusion in her path. One day, she stormed right through the waiting room and barricaded herself with a steel folding chair in the break room. I came to collect her and gently opened the door, not knowing she had haplessly placed the chair under the door handle. As she sat waiting for me with her head buried in her arms, the steel chair fell suddenly to the floor with a crash that sent both Agnes and me jumping in spontaneous fright.

One of the ironic things about Agnes's transparent attempts at manipulation was her unerring ability to succeed in scaring and startling us. Once we had both recovered a normal heart rate and the chair was returned to its upright position, we went back to my office, Agnes glaring at me unflinchingly. I was sure she thought I had somehow planned the whole loud commotion for her humiliation.

Once we closed the door, she kicked off her worn out shoes and stretched out on the couch. Agnes was one of only three people who has ever come in and reclined on my couch, despite the popular concept about therapists and their sofas. The other two were chronic pain patients.

"I should never have been born!" she scoffed. "My retarded parents made a big mistake when they brought me into this world. Jesus! My dad was a fool to even marry my mother. And you know my mother." Agnes paused and leaned forward from her reclining position on the couch. She cupped her hand toward the side of her mouth and whispered, "She is a total B-I-T-C-H, you know."

Then sitting back, her wrath turned theological. "And don't even get me started on . . . that Thing!" she said, shaking her fist skyward. Her disdain for God was clear and she refused to call God anything except "Thing!" "If this keeps up, I'll stab my own funeral director!" she closed, not worrying about the impossibility of such an event.

Adrift diagnostically, I turned my attention to the analysis of transference. This concept is a classic feature of the psychotherapeutic endeavor. Transference refers to the patient's unresolved interpersonal conflict which is brought to the session and projected onto the therapist. This was indeed an adventure all its own with Agnes.

The same erratic affect she displayed with regard to her parents was increasingly demonstrated toward me. When she was angry, I was perceived as taunting her with my questions, manipulating her affections, and plotting to separate her parents from their money. When she was not angry, she was altogether different. I was not sure which presentation was more unnerving. In the latter state, Agnes did everything but declare her love for me directly.

Contrary to the practice of many therapists, I chose to wear my wedding ring during sessions. The practice of not wearing a ring may come from the desire to encourage transference by remaining as ambiguous as possible, and wearing a ring is considered too personal and self-disclosing. But my ring did not inhibit Agnes. She never even let on that she was aware of it. She spoke as if I were single. At one point she did ask if I was married, but before I could answer, she cut me off. "Please, don't tell me if you are. I think it would break my heart," she blurted.

She sometimes flirted outrageously, batting her eyes and dramatically feigning a blush. She would ask me to hold her hand, a request I gently declined. At other times, she lay back languorously on the couch, pointing her toes demurely.

One session, she brought me a picture of the model Claudia Schiffer from a magazine, reporting it to be a picture of her when she was a younger woman, before such hard times. She honestly thought I would believe her. I wasn't sure that she might not actually believe it herself. Was this a true delusion?

I decided to reply directly, "Gee, Agnes, you must be mistaken. I believe this is a picture of a well-known model named Claudia Schiffer." She snatched the magazine back, looked at the picture, and after a moment sheepishly offered an explanation. "No, I meant that I used to look like this woman when I was younger."

About eighteen months into our work together, I came to realize, much later than I should have, what I believed to be the source of Agnes's problems. At the core, we were talking about her grief that she had once been a pretty girl with a big world of opportunities open to her.

"But then when I was fourteen, it all went to hell," she said sadly. A cryptic statement of three words, "That damn truck!" finished her reflection.

What truck? I thought. Had she been in an accident? Had she been kidnapped? My imagination was running wild. "Agnes, what truck?"

"The truck with all the flies," she said. "That's when my parents put me in that terrible place."

Had she been abused in some institution? Had she been beaten? Had she been sexually assaulted?

"I lost it. That is when the dream died," she said, puzzling me more.

After I prodded her further, Agnes finally gave me in a minute what I had been trying for over a year to understand.

"I was fourteen when my parents called the cops and had me taken to the nut house."

"You were hospitalized?" I asked. "Why did your parents have you admitted to the hospital?"

"They saw me chasing the garbage truck down the street," she said. "I was barking at it like a dog."

The mystery was finally solved. Agnes had had her first psychotic break and been hospitalized when she was fourteen.

Although the psychosis had apparently resolved, she was never able to return to the childhood that had been so harshly interrupted. However, she was not so impaired that she could not keenly remember it, and she pined for the innocent child she once had been.

Sadly forced by insurance companies to make diagnoses, I made a decision about a diagnosis for Agnes, Mixed Personality Disorder with Histrionic, Borderline, and Paranoid Features. But beyond any category or list of criteria, Agnes demonstrated one inflexible characteristic. She appeared entirely self-absorbed by her own pain and calamity. She never asked about my feelings or gave any awareness that she knew I had feelings. At times I was amazed at how callous she could be. If some catastrophic natural disaster was in the news, she would come into the session absolutely distraught, not with distress over what had happened to others, but because of the certainty that a similar tragedy would strike her.

Well into our second year, I began to despair that I might never find a way to reach behind that fortress of pain. I was doubting myself and I was doubting her. Fear set in that we had been wasting our time with nothing to show for our work. After two years and more than a hundred sessions, she was as lost and angry as ever.

Many clinicians consider it unethical to encourage an intermittently psychotic person to reflect and look inward. Psychotherapy, by its very nature, seeks insight, but those who hallucinate and are delusional are often unsettled by such a process. While Agnes never appeared to hallucinate or have fixed delusions, she certainly had her own ways of distorting and playing with reality. Was I harming her by continuing to see her?

Based on these fears, I began to look for some way to wrap up the therapy, but Agnes, ever vigilant, would launch into a broken tirade about how she couldn't handle the rejection if I ever dropped her case. I felt pity for her circumstance, but I had no idea how to compassionately communicate that to her. Her defenses formed an impenetrable wall that prevented us from truly engaging one another in a meaningful way.

Late in December, I came to our session preoccupied by my 17-month-old daughter Abigail's sudden life-threatening medical emergency. She had contracted a rare strain of pneumonia that was extremely resistant to antibiotics. It had started with a common virus that was going around, and this complication had emerged. She had run fevers of one-hundred-and-five degrees on and off for several days, and by the time the pathogen was identified, the upper two lobes of her left lung were completely consolidated with fluid. She was evacuated by air to Fort Worth's Cook Children's Hospital. I rode with Abby in the airplane and helplessly watched as her fever spiked again. Over the previous 48 hours, my wife and I had noticed her weakening. She was a fighter, but she was losing strength with every breath. She lay completely limp, her body focusing all its strength on the task of trying to breathe.

The doctors at the hospital had told us that Abby would either turn a corner soon, or they would have to put her on a ventilator. We had watched her rally over the next few days only to weaken. We would become hopeful with every sign of improvement, then lapse into despair when she went through a low time.

After about two weeks in the hospital, she stabilized. "Not out of the woods yet," the doctors said cautiously. "We may have to do surgery, but we won't know for a few days."

One of the downsides to private practice and being your own boss is that there is no "Family Leave Act." I had taken several days off already and desperately needed to get back to keep the practice going. After discussion, my wife and I decided that I should go home until we learned if surgery was going to be necessary.

Exhausted and a bit shell-shocked, I had arrived at the office that morning to find Agnes scheduled at ten o'clock. I was dreading dealing with her antics. I suspected she would be angry and feel rejected because I had canceled our last appointment due to my being at the hospital.

In this expectation I was not wrong. Agnes was in the full tilt of rage.

"Where were you the last two weeks?" she demanded. "You are so heartless. You know how much I need these sessions. You obviously don't give a tinker's damn about me."

Finally, she leaned forward and shouted at me, "I have to have my sessions, man!"

Frustrated and lost, I thought, Why am I doing this to both of us? She can't possibly understand what I'm going through. Look at her. She is shaking, rambling, fragmented and tortured in her thoughts. She wouldn't know the difference if I told her I was the President of the United States and had a national security emergency!

Probably out of frustration, I broke one of my own rules. In keeping with the practice of limiting self-disclosure, I had never told her I was married or whether or not I had children. But when she demanded to know why I had missed our appointment, I simply told her the truth.

"Agnes," I began, interrupting her fuming. "I have never told you much about myself, but I guess it's time. I have a wife and three children. My youngest, Abby, is just a year-and-a-half old. She is blond-headed and blue-eyed, and she has the sweetest smile I have ever seen. And this morning, she is sick—very sick. She is at Cook Children's Hospital in Fort Worth. Her mother and I have been watching after her day and night. And that is why I missed our last appointments."

Truthfully, I hadn't told Agnes about Abby to try to elicit sympathy. Agnes had shown no capacity for that. Inducing guilt had not been my objective either. I was not so much a therapist in that moment as I was a tired, worried father and an exhausted psychologist who was giving up on a client he had failed to reach, and giving up hope that he ever would.

Sitting there in a daze, lost in my sorry thoughts, I realized that silence had descended on us both. That had never happened with us.

Awareness of the silence, novel in the tortuous history of our work together, snapped me back to our session, and to Agnes.

To my amazement, Agnes herself seemed to be changing, transforming before me in a matter of seconds. Her eyes, which out of shame and self-deprecation, had met mine only in anger over the past two years, locked onto me with a softness I had never seen in her before. She gently bit her lower lip and gave me what had previously been impossible, her undivided attention. That long silence I can only describe as impossibly intimate.

What came next was one of those moments when noxious pain or suffering is overwhelmed by the sweet and far more powerful fragrance of grace.

Agnes, the tortured, fragmented, angry, and lost soul, got up slowly from her seat and approached me. The last time she had done this had nearly scared me to death, but this time I could not have been more comfortable. She walked over to the side of my chair and lowered her face. I wondered if she wanted to whisper something to me. But she continued to bow until her face was just below my chin. Then, she gently laid her head on my chest. She stayed there for a minute, pressing her face into my chest, tears of compassion rolling down her face. Agnes was showing me compassion, and I was beginning to see how beautiful she really was.

Coda:

It is so difficult to render the stories of psychotherapy without risking exploitation of the patient and abuse of the therapist-client relationship. I have never struggled with this issue as much as I have with my work with Agnes. Originally, I wrote this because I couldn't help myself; I had to. But I also thought I had to keep it private and not let anyone else read it. My feelings about Agnes and my description of her in the early part of my story were frank and honest, but also an honest reflection of my own prejudices and bigotry. I had harshly and wrongly judged Agnes. How could I ever reveal such a hurtful opinion to anyone without harming her?

I left the story in a drawer for over a decade when, without warning, Agnes came back into my life. She was grieving the loss of her mother and the rapid decline in her father's health. Many things had not changed. Agnes was still disheveled and rambling, but I didn't know whether to break into laughter or tears when I realized how much I had missed her, in all of her unique, hilarious, tragic "Agnes"-ness.

I listened to her broken heart and her paranoia as she told me about the years that had passed since we had last seen each other. I wondered what she even remembered about our work so long ago. As the session drew to a close, I felt compelled to make a confession.

"Agnes, after we concluded our work together, I wrote about you and me and all we went through together back then."

Agnes' eyebrows raised in surprise. "You did? You wrote about me?"

"Yes, I never showed it to anyone, but I wanted you to know our work together meant a great deal to me. I am not sure I ever helped you back then, but I want to thank you for helping me in a difficult time."

"Gosh, Doc, I never helped anyone in my whole life. You're just saying that."

"No, it's true. I wrote about it."

Agnes' brow furrowed for a moment before her eyes widened, "Would you read it to me?"

With some trepidation, I went to my desk and took out the story. At first, I thought I would try to skip over the parts that might be hurtful. But that would not be easy without affecting the story, and maybe that wouldn't be honest. So, I simply read it to her straight up—all of it.

When I finished, I looked up, not knowing what she might say. She had tears rolling down her cheeks toward her broad smile. "That's about me, man! I love it!" she said. "Can I have a copy of it? I would love to have a copy."

Agnes waited downstairs while I made a copy for her. Afterwards, we wandered out onto the veranda outside my office. "Good-bye, Agnes. Come see me again if you need to," I said sincerely.

She took the copy of the story in her arms, clutching it to her chest.

"I will," she said smiling. "I will."

chapter six

NOTES FROM THE INFERNO

JANUARY 28, 2010

David,

I thought I would give you an update on my disease. Since coming home to Scotland, my condition has deteriorated. I no longer have any use of my right leg and much of my left. Falling has become a daily thing, and I must admit I do it well. Therefore, I am wheelchair confined and home bound. I also spend much of my time dysfunctional in bed.

I had been looking forward to Christmas as my family was going to my brother and sister-in-law's house. Unfortunately, I fell twice during the early morning hours of Christmas Day and was unable to get out of bed. They did come to see about me that day, but it wasn't the same. For the first time ever, I hit rock bottom. I figured out I had not left the house since October and I spend ninety-five percent of my time alone and in desperate pain. I have decided the quality of my life is unacceptable.

I have come up with a possible option. My sixtieth birthday is April 24, so I made this my deadline. I asked my sister for a birthday party. I enrolled the help of my closest friends and my brother and my pain management doctor. The idea is to set dates for movies, meals out, and meetings for coffee. My pain doctor is going to review my meds and wants my physical needs to be reassessed. So this is my plan. I don't want to die, but I can't live like this.

Let me know what you think, not as a professional, but as my friend. Thank you and I hope you and yours are well.

All the best,

Betty

January 29, 2010

Betty,

I am so sorry. I am going to start the chapter about you and me in the next couple of days. The suicide option has been out there a long time, and I suspect it has brought you comfort at times. But I also know you have been passionate about the plight of pain patients, in particular those who suffer with Reflex Sympathetic Dystrophy.

Perhaps there is meaning in seeing this chapter through with me. If you trust my voice to share your story, our story, it may give some purpose to the terrible pain you are dealing with, at least for now.

Please know, however, that I have come to trust your wisdom about your life, and as a friend, I believe you deserve to write the story of your life your way, and that includes its conclusion. Also, I would like to be there for you in whatever way I can. My thoughts and prayers are with you.

David

The psychotherapist is generally the sworn enemy of suicide. One of our core values is that life is worth living. And in spite of the undeniable fact that life often has pain, it is also beautiful, precious, and full of joy.

The psychotherapist is generally the sworn enemy of suicide. One of our core values is that life is worth living.

In these years, I have been able to get up and go to work confident in my faith in these cardinal beliefs. Then came Betty.

March 11, 1998

The day Betty first came to see me, she was on crutches, and she winced as she hobbled through the door of the office. My personal office is on the second floor, but patients who can't climb the stairs meet with me in the room with the fireplace and a wall of books. The "library," as we call it, was the space where Betty and I would meet weekly for the next few years.

Leaning forward on her crutches at the reception window, the 50- year -old, medically-retired nurse/educator with a Scottish brogue, whispered to the staff, "Is Doctor Sabine a man?"

"Yes ma'am," replied the secretary.

"That's good," she said, with a hint of the mischievous in her grin. "Is he cute?"

The secretary was so caught off guard by the question, she turned a bit red in the face.

Betty was good-natured in her laughter at the poor girl's speechless reaction.

"It's okay, honey," she continued in her conspiratorial tone. "I'll decide that for myself."

In a few minutes, I invited her into the library.

"Good morning, Betty. What brings us together?"

"Do you know what RSD is?" she asked curtly.

"Yes, I do," I replied.

"Tell me what you know," she said, peering over the top of her glasses.

Feeling a bit like I was being given a test, I told her that it was my understanding that Reflex Sympathetic Dystrophy is a chronic pain condition also referred to as "Neuralgia." Its cause is largely mysterious, confounding attempts at medical treatment, but it seems to come on quite unpredictably. Sometimes it comes in the wake of trauma, sometimes even a minor injury, and is characterized by chronic, progressive, and incurable pain. The pain may start in an extremity and over time migrate to involve the entire limb and sometimes ultimately involving other limbs as well. The pain from this condition is difficult to describe, sometimes burning, sometimes throbbing, and sometimes suddenly stabbing, like a knife in the affected limb. The tissue becomes bright red and hot to the touch, if the patient can tolerate touch at all. Sometimes just the brush of clothing across the skin can be excruciating.

Over time, the use of the limb may be lost, as much due to atrophy as anything. If the disorder is diagnosed within the first six months of manifest symptoms, it may be managed or cured. But if not, the sufferer often does not recover and must cope with the chronic pain.

"Not bad," Betty said after my summary. "You'd be surprised how many doctors have never heard of it."

"I guess it is fairly obscure," I said. "I just happen to have worked with chronic pain patients in grad school. I also ran the chronic pain program at the rehab hospital for a couple of years, so I have worked with patients with RSD a few times. I'm no expert, but I am familiar with it."

When Betty approved of my expertise, I smiled, feeling a little pleased with myself that I was surviving the audition.

"One other thing."

"What's that?" I asked.

"I can't deal with this 'doctor' crap. Can I call you 'David?'"

"Of course," I said.

And with that, we launched into the session in earnest.

Betty was an accomplished nurse, working for years in different clinical settings, and ultimately becoming the director of the nurse training program at the local community college. She had to retire because of her pain. She was tough and demanded excellence from herself, her staff, and especially her students. Her lyrical brogue added punch to every quip and clever turn of phrase, but it could cut close too, revealing she was a woman to be reckoned with.

One of the challenges of working with Betty was the intersection of the person and the pathology. She was irascible, charming, funny, and very bright. But RSD, her tenacious adversary, is a well-oiled pain machine, sporting an arsenal stocked with all of the sharp and probing tools of torture. In spite of her admirable gifts of optimism and persistence, she was no match for this relentless affliction.

Quite accomplished, she was also agonizingly independent. She would rather suffer alone than feel she was putting someone out. In fact, she rarely risked talking to her family back in Scotland, fearing they would view her complaining about pain as a tacit request to come home and be taken care of by them all.

That she could not abide. So, the support and understanding that she might conceivably elicit from people who cared about her were shut out. I couldn't decide if Betty's distancing herself from her family was based in her own issues or theirs, but probably both.

Through my years of working with patients, I have come to handle some of the pains of life more effectively. I am not as fearful of death as I used to be. Death is a portal to mystery, and I have come to trust the Mystery of Life. I have a sneaking suspicion that what lies on the other side of the portal is benign, perhaps even sublime. I used to avoid interpersonal conflict at all costs, but I now recognize it as an important and promising fact of life that is often a catalyst to change. Separation, solitude, divorce, estrangement from loved ones, all have the capacity to wound deeply and for a while may seem insurmountable, but in time, they can be approached and overcome. Healing can happen, and the problems can occasionally even be understood as important turning points in life. We may each come to the rather startling epiphany that we are actually a better person because of, not in spite of, what we have been through.

However, I must admit that chronic, unremitting, unmanageable pain still terrifies me. When I have to deal with acute pain, I am comforted by the fact that I know it will not last forever. I can bear it until it passes. I can take pain medication that, at the very least, takes the edge off. Finally, I am comforted by the attention and care of people who love me and rush to my aid. Even if they cannot exorcise it, they will stay with me until the worst of it passes. It might be an inconvenience for them, but it is short-lived. I will be better soon and we can all go back to our usual, relatively pain-free lives.

But for Betty and thousands of others like her, this is not true. After living with this unrelenting pain for twelve years, she had every reason to believe that it would stalk her for the rest of her life. No cure is in sight. Even when physicians and researchers talk about one, which is seldom, they refer to the hope for those who are newly diagnosed, not those with advanced RSD. "Hope," typically one of the most cherished of human sensibilities, had turned on Betty. She created more new ways and reasons to hope than anybody I had ever known. When five years had rolled by, she waited five more, but the hope for a cure always turned out to be another cruel hoax.

After watching Betty's suffering, I was humbled knowing I couldn't bear her pain for an hour. I might try to take it on for a day if Betty were to stay with me and tell me how to cope. Unbelievably, she was fast approaching 5,000 days in pain. One of my first questions for God, if I get the chance to ask, will be why did Betty have to suffer this way? I am angry and heart-broken when I think about it.

Pain medication had become another cruelty. It had dulled the pain, but the price in side effects was high. To get even mild relief, Betty had to take enough that she became lethargic and numb, unable to experience much joy in life at all. She was unsteady and fell with alarming frequency, probably hundreds of times. Sometimes she would come to the office and we would try to have a session, but she would be so sedated that she could not participate meaningfully and we would have to reschedule.

One of her dear friends, Barbara, would take Betty the 150 miles from Wichita Falls to her pain doctor in Dallas. The trip in the car was so painful that Betty would have to knock herself out entirely to make it. Barbara would put Betty in the back seat and stuff pillows around her. On one such trip, Barbara had to brake suddenly.

Barbara recalls: "After I came to a stop, I looked in the rearview mirror that I had turned down so I could watch Betty in the back. Horrified, I saw that she was gone! I looked frantically over the seat to see that Betty had rolled face down in the floorboard of the back seat. I was afraid she couldn't breathe. The cars behind me kept honking, so I was driving through Dallas, trying to find a place to stop before Betty was suffocated."

Thus, Betty had to make a dreadful choice between being aware of life but in excruciating pain, or being semi-comatose to the point where time would be lost, memory would be blank, and life would be a passing blur.

Perhaps one of the cruelest aspects of chronic pain is the way it isolates you from the care of others. In one classic study, test subjects were given a stop watch and asked to go alone into a room and submerge their bare foot in ice water. They were asked to record how long they could make themselves endure the pain before they had to withdraw their foot. Then, the same procedure was followed again, only this time another person was sent in with the subject to hold the stopwatch. Remarkably, the researchers found that if someone else was with the subject, the amount of time they could endure the pain doubled!

Another study demonstrated that if pain is predictable, it can be coped with much more easily. It is not experienced as severely as when it is random and unpredictable.

For people who suffer chronic pain, the tension in the face so often seen in acute pain is absent. With no outward sign of distress, the sufferers must often tolerate suspicions at best, and accusations at worst, that they are not really in pain at all, just seeking attention or faking. This only adds another sad layer of pain, this time being seen as a fraud. Social support can evaporate just when it's most needed.

Support is labor-intensive, most effective when it is short-lived.

Even those who mean well are often frustrated and end up distancing. When someone is in acute pain, friends and relatives gather around and support the person until the pain is resolved. But support is labor-intensive, most effective when it is short-lived. With chronic pain, however, those who love the person often burn themselves out in traditional, but ineffective, methods of support. In fact, being overly solicitous and rescuing the patient from having to do things he or she can still adequately do has a destructive effect, hastening debility and atrophy.

Ninety-five percent of the time, Betty was "living", if you could call it that, alone. When she would try to get up, she would fall. The pain meds were sedating her, making her life bland and out of focus. What meaning is there in a life like this? Imagining yourself in such a situation, what would you do to cope? Would you be tempted to look for a way out?

Suicide's seductive song began to call to Betty about three years into our work together. She spoke often of the idea. As a nurse, she knew what medications to take to accomplish the deed. The medications she was already taking were lethal if taken in excess. She would only have to squirrel away a few pills for a month or two. No one would be the wiser. Betty also prided herself as a woman of courage. If she decided to end her life, she would not falter because of fear. The idea of suicide did not make her at all squeamish.

When I took the place prescribed by my profession, standing between my patient, Betty, and what she considered her last hope for escape, it was with a quiet and troubling ambivalence. First, I wondered if there is such a thing as "rational suicide," a descriptive term coined by Thomas Szasz over thirty years ago. Was suicide always an act of a disturbed mind, or can it be a legitimate expression of one's own autonomy? Can choosing to die in certain circumstances be a dignified way to take responsibility for one's own life?

I had read the work of Szasz in graduate school, but then it had seemed an academic and philosophical exercise, calling on one to speculate about the logical end of the argument for life. But here, in working with Betty, the question was no longer an academic, philosophical meandering. It was, instead, a life and death matter, unfolding with stark clarity as the days passed.

The customary way to deal with a suicidal patient, if hospitalization is not appropriate, is with a so-called "contract for safety." There are several steps to the contract, but the central point is that if the patient begins to feel suicidal, he or she will call the therapist before taking any action to cause self-harm.

I had made the customary contract with Betty without incident in our first session. She knew the drill. We would review the contract from time to time whenever the pain exploded and the lure of escape and relief tempted her to let go and give in.

Several years into our work together, the contract itself became the content of our discussion.

"David, I have a question about the contract." Betty confided. "If I do get to the place where I am planning to kill myself, and I make that call we keep bringing up, you know that I won't be going to a psych hospital. What are you going to say to me?"

In all the contracts for safety I had ever made, this question had never been asked. Several easy answers came to mind, but I had long ago made the commitment to Betty to shoot straight and stick close to the data my own heart recorded. And although I felt exposed and on the spot by her question, the moment was surprisingly intimate. There was no posture of challenge or confrontation. This was not a test. Betty really wanted to know.

I told her the unadorned truth.

"I don't know what I'll say, Betty," I told her. "I just want my shot if that time comes."

Betty paused, looking at me for a moment and seeming to take a measure of some intangible thing in me.

"Fair enough," she said, nodding. "Fair enough."

Time rolled on. The children continued to grow up. My eldest graduated from high school. My youngest laid down the million miles of toddlerhood under his mother's watchful eye. Each year or two, we loaded up with friends and sailed the string of jewels called the British Virgin Islands. The struggles of my life seemed to be about the problem of balancing so many great blessings. If I could just avoid getting stuck too obsessively in one of the many things l loved, I might be able to avoid sabotaging a pretty good life.

> *If I could just avoid getting stuck too obsessively in one of the many things I loved, I might be able to avoid sabotaging a pretty good life.*

Meanwhile, day after interminable day Betty continued in inexorable pain. She was usually alone except for the company of a few kind friends who checked in on her and helped her get to her doctors' appointments. But most days began and ended in pain and solitude, interrupted only by the occasional delirium of narcotic medication. Her only excursions from her home were to medical offices, brief paroles before more solitary confinement.

Unfortunately, the medical and insurance systems provided more aggravations. Even before we had started working together, her medical treatment had been an adventure. Betty's doctors had implanted a spinal cord stimulator. When pain medication seems to become ineffective, spinal cord stimulators are an option. The small devices have electrodes placed "upstream" from the aggravating nerve, and the battery pack is implanted under the skin. Sometimes, the process offers a degree of relief for the chronic pain sufferer. But instead of relief, Betty came perilously close to dying from complications of the procedure itself. Instead of pain relief, all she had to show for it was a new pacemaker, needed to regulate her damaged heart. In another layer of irony and bad fortune, that same pacemaker would later make her ineligible for a promising experimental treatment for RSD.

She had also endured countless nerve block injections aimed at giving her a few weeks of pain relief. They were impotent in the face of her enemy.

When Betty first came to see me, she was being seen by Dr. Scott, a pain management specialist in Wichita Falls who was very dear to her. She said he listened to her and worked with her in managing her pain. Although he was not particularly successful in finding her a lasting relief, he seemed to really empathize with her plight. In fact, he took it personally when the pain did not abate. He was always in an upbeat mood and had a playful sense of humor. While some people might think that physicians who deal in the grim business of human misery every day would eventually become either broken by the experience or numb to their patient's complaints, Dr. Scott appeared immune to those failings. He remained a stalwart source of encouragement in Betty's purgatory.

"Besides," she said, "he's so damn cute."

For a while, the arrangement with Dr. Scott and myself as Betty's primary pain management team seemed to work, if not to relieve the pain, then at least to help her cope with it.

Then came the letter from Dr. Scott.

One morning, Betty arrived for her session, rolled her wheelchair up to the table in the library, pulled out an envelope stuffed beside her, and threw it down in front of me. "Check that out," she said.

It was from Dr. Scott. He explained that he was quitting as a physician provider for the Worker's Compensation Fund. The Fund had made a new requirement that doctors go to a training program to be eligible for compensation. There would be no "grandfather clause," and every doctor had to do the training on his or her own dime. Dr. Scott's letter stated that seeing worker's comp patients would now be cost prohibitive. Sadly, Betty was receiving medical treatment under worker's compensation.

In my years of practice as a psychologist, I have never seen a system as broken as the Texas Worker's Compensation Fund. Even though I still work with patients who are under the fund, the casework involved makes my staff and me grimace. Medically necessary care will often be denied outright by case reviewers. But the Fund's more subtle and equally pernicious strategy is to delay. Authorization for service takes forever, and if a doctor is lucky enough to get it, he or she will have to write letters by the score and send documentation of the documentation to the point of exhaustion. On the left side of Betty's chart, I have archived all of the letters I have written for her case. The archive is several inches thick.

Betty's assigned adjuster was named Dwayne. I did not know him personally, and I was confident that he must possess some redeemable qualities. By the time he was assigned to Betty's case, however, he had them well hidden, perhaps because too many people were trying to scam the system.

Dwayne seemed unfazed by Betty's requests for equipment and services and by my considerable efforts to impress upon him the legitimacy of her plight. He seemed to feel a perverse delight in saying "no" to whatever the need. Betty came to say his name like she was referring to a poisonous snake. She would sneer and spit out "Dwayne" as if it were something distasteful.

But the day Dr. Scott's letter arrived, an entirely new and diabolically effective method of denying care was announced. The requirement of extra training was just what was needed for physicians, already burdened by the low compensation and logistical nightmare of Worker's Comp, to opt out. In fact, ninety percent of the doctors in Wichita Falls who had taken Worker's Comp quit taking new cases and fired all of their current "comp" patients. The two or three remaining doctors who were willing to do the training to remain providers were inundated with 300 new patients requesting service. The result was chaos.

Betty's case was so complex and taxing that none of the local doctors left in the Comp system would touch her. She now had to go a hundred and fifty miles just to get to a doctor who would treat her.

The relationship with Dr. Scott, who had been such a source of hope and encouragement to her, was over. She had been fired and she never saw him again. Instead of being angry at Dr. Scott, she was sympathetic. Her anger was correctly directed at the Fund, still as broken now, a decade later, as it was then.

A few years after the letter, Dr. Scott's own life tragically unraveled. He was found in his office dead by his own hand. Even though Betty had not seen him since the letter, she still found the news of his death difficult. She hadn't been under his care, but she had still taken comfort in knowing he was always pulling for her. And now he was gone.

Inpatient treatment was next for Betty. After a year or two of outpatient management working to give Betty psychological strategies for handling her pain, her adjustors decided Betty needed an inpatient chronic pain program.

Having worked in a few of these programs in the past, I thought this was a reasonable step. While I didn't know the particular program to which she was headed, the adjusters reassured both of us that she would receive comprehensive treatment.

Betty disappeared into her program for a few weeks. As her first appointment with me after her return came near, I was eager to hear how it had gone. However, when she returned, she gave no indication in her countenance how she was doing.

"Betty, it's great to see you. Tell me about your experience in treatment. How did it go?"

Betty looked over her glasses at me, and I knew things had not gone well. "All I can say, David, is what a crock. I never thought I would miss the often-dreaded four walls of my own room, but that I did. I feel like I have been a prisoner for thirty days. The first thing they did was declare me a drug addict, and then they stuck me on a general psych ward with all the garden variety loonies."

"I thought this was a dedicated pain management program," I said.

"Ha!" she said. "More like a detox and drug rehab. It is obvious they know nothing about my disease."

She went on to lament that instead of a specialist in pain management, she had been under the care of a psychiatrist. Her own personal "Cuckoo's Nest" experience had been a physical and emotional nightmare.

Luckily, Betty did not shrink or fade away when she wasn't getting what she actually needed for her care. Again and again, she inundated Dwayne and his supervisors with requests. She became a master at all their arcane rules and runarounds. Each request that was made required certain actions be taken in a certain time frame, each more ingenious than the last. Inevitably, the requests were still met with rejection.

My favorite story was Betty's response to a denial by the Comp Fund regarding a request for a motorized wheel chair.

"David, I finally got word from *Dwayne* on my wheel chair," she said, almost gagging on his name. "He denied me."

"Crap, Betty. I hate that," I said.

"Well, I think he balked because of the expense. It's about five thousand dollars," she responded.

"That is one pricey ride," I said, astonished.

"Well, he's going to love my new request. This morning, I sent out another one for a custom van with wheel chair lift and special access steering and shifting mechanisms."

She said this with her patented Betty-look-of-mischief.

"Okay," I said with a smile. "How much is that gonna cost?"

"About fifty thousand, I think. I figure that might just make my Dwayne swallow his tongue." Betty's get-even spunk was so familiar. Over the next few months, she chased that van like she fully expected it to show up in her driveway any day. Dwayne was required to respond to every request.

The van never showed up, nor did the wheel chair or anything else that might have really made a measurable difference in the quality of her life.

Betty wanted to write a book about her experiences with life, pain, and the world of "Comp." She wanted to make a difference for all of the other people marginalized by a system that appeared to be designed to doubt the validity of their pain or disability. But alas and again, her pain prevented her from doing that, too.

One night, around two in the morning, my pager went off. I am on call all the time, but my patients respect that my pager is for emergencies, so it almost never sounds off at night. When the night call came, I felt the cold touch of dread as I saw Betty's number displayed on the pager. I bolted upright on the edge of the bed, grabbed the phone and dialed her number.

"David, I'm sorry to page you in the middle of the night," she said when I answered.

"Don't worry about that" I said. "Tell me what's wrong."

In a clear and calm voice, her words came through the receiver: "This is your call."

We sat in silence for a few seconds. This is it, I thought. Betty has come to the point where she can't handle the pain. *What was I going to say?* I had gotten similar calls before from other despondent patients. Each time, I had helped get the patient into the hospital. I knew Betty's call was not a tacit agreement to be hospitalized, after her horrible experience in the psych hospital. She was putting a different question to me. *"Why should I go on?"*

I had never been in a pain like Betty's, so I couldn't speculate if I could bear it. However, if I forced the issue and called the police to her house, would I be doing a compassionate thing in preserving her life, or would I instead be compelling her to suffer on, this time without *choosing* to live, but being forced to march on?

No, Betty was not calling me to instigate a hospitalization. Nor was she calling for a clever argument, or a pep talk to get her back into bearing the suffering. She was calling on *me*, trusting the relationship we had built together over time to see if I could be a light in her moment in her despair.

"Betty, we have talked about this moment many times, haven't we?" I said.

"Many times, David. Finally, we are here. What is your answer?"

"The truth is, Betty, that I don't have an argument for you about why you should go on. I don't profess to know what the answer is. But I want to say, if you go, I will miss you. I have come to know a world with you in it, and if you are not here, it will matter to me. I know you would not have called had hope not failed you tonight, but I still have hope for you. I believe there may be good reasons to stay, even though neither of us knows just now what they are. But I commit to you that I will stay with you. We will search high and low for a better answer for you."

Silence descended again, but the quiet was different. After a few seconds, I heard "Thank you, David. I will think about that. Now go back to bed. I'll see you later." And with that the line went dead.

I hung up, but my heart was racing and tears were rolling down my face. It appeared that Betty was going to stay for the time being, and I hoped she would not regret that decision.

That was four years ago. Betty carried on. In fact, she made changes which I thought she might never be capable of making. I had feared that the stubbornness that kept her alive also isolated her. I had known she was loath to worry her family about her condition. So I was naturally surprised when she came into session a few weeks after our crisis and informed me she was thinking about going home to Scotland.

"I think that's great, Betty. I'm sure your family would love for you to come home. A visit from you after all this time would be great."

"I'm not talking about a visit, David. I'm considering the idea of moving back home."

I was thunderstruck. Betty could barely make it to Dallas under heavy sedation. How could she make that trip and how could she move all her belongings with her? And what about her family? Would they be willing and able to help? She had been so secretive about her suffering.

I should have known not to worry. Betty is extraordinary, with a will of steel. Over the next few months, she set about the logistics of getting her things moved. She had her family arrange a house for her to move into when she arrived. She had the reams of medical records released to the team of physicians who awaited her arrival.

As the time approached for her departure, I anticipated a growing feeling of loss. Betty, her life and her suffering, had become important to me. While boundaries are critical to good work in psychotherapy, Betty had, through her humor and her courage, insinuated herself into my heart. She had forgiven my failings and imperfections.

While boundaries are critical to good work in psychotherapy, Betty had, through her humor and her courage, insinuated herself into my heart.

Betty and I both had hoped our work together would result in a fruitful way for her to cope with her pain. But for some reason I still don't fully understand, in spite of what seemed like her best effort, she did not find a great deal of relief in those strategies. Perhaps I am just not as competent at teaching pain management techniques as I thought. Maybe I didn't follow through with them properly. Such self-doubts still haunt me.

My last session with Betty took place just a couple of days before she flew back to Scotland. We reviewed all our work together. She thanked me for helping and I thanked her for inspiring me with her courage. We talked about coping skills for the inevitable stress that would come from the transition she was about to undergo. And then, with a hug, ever so gentle to not exacerbate a nerve and roil her pain, we said good-bye.

Several weeks went by before I heard anything from Betty. At last, I got an e-mail from her. Although the pain was still unabated, she sounded upbeat and grateful for the new life she was undertaking in Scotland. She thanked me again.

I didn't hear from her often after that. The therapeutic boundaries involved were on my mind. What if Betty went into crisis again? What could I do from Texas if she needed help? Did corresponding with her imply that a therapeutic relationship and responsibility was still in place? Many might say that I should just reaffirm the boundary and afford her the privilege of taking care of herself, that talking to her or writing represented a dual relationship, which is simply forbidden.

While I did respond a time or two, I kept the correspondence brief. I intimated that I was still sympathetic to her struggles, but I did not inquire into her present situation very deeply, or offer ideas about how to handle situations she faced. I felt awkward and guilty for not doing more, but I had to respect professional boundaries.

In 2008, my son-in-law's beloved grandfather died in England, and I traveled to the funeral. As the train raced north out of London on the way to Wolverhampton, I realized that I was only five or six hours away from Betty's Scottish home. I felt strange to be that close and not seek her, but again, I decided that leaving the relationship as it was best served both our interests.

February 25, 2010

The letter from Betty at the beginning of this story came just over a month ago. I don't know, of course, what, if anything, will happen on Betty's 60th birthday. But after hearing Betty's story, what would you tell her? Would you counsel that she cannot opt for ending her life intentionally? That it would be unethical for her to take her own life regardless of the circumstances? Is the desire for death always a function of mental illness or is there such a thing as a rational, moral suicide?

As I sat in my ethics class in graduate school, this issue seemed pretty cut and dried for me. Life is always worth living, and its end is up to God, or Life, or whatever. We just didn't have the right to enter into that conversation with another person. It is beyond our role.

> *Is the desire for death always a function of mental illness or is there such a thing as a rational, moral suicide?*

But here I am, in that very conversation with Betty. You can make a case that I am co-dependent with her and that we have an enmeshed relationship. That could be true, but I don't think that is the definitive problem. During our time together, I have come to genuinely love Betty and hope for the best for her. I would be safer sticking to the party line and defending the value of life at any cost. But if my years of working with people have taught me anything, it is that when it comes to love, there is no such thing as a safe distance.

> *If my years of working with people have taught me anything, it is that when it comes to love, there is no such thing as a safe distance.*

I don't mean that boundaries should therefore be thrown out. They are one of the best ways we love others. But there are times when the vagaries of life redraw the boundaries, and this is one of those times. Betty's concerns about continuing her life are legitimate and grounded in truth. From me, she does not deserve the preachment or condescension that so often accompanies the appeal to ethical principles. After all she has been through, she deserves the respect afforded by affirming her right to live her life on her terms. As I have said in my letter to her, that includes the right to write the final chapter.

And so, my telling of Betty's story, my challenges and rewards in our heartbreaking relationship, ends here. She, not I, will have the last word.

CHASING SHAME: CONCERTO FOR PIANO– INTRODUCTION TO CHAPTERS SEVEN THROUGH NINE

WHEN I COMPLETED my Ph.D. in 1993, I bought myself a graduation present –a six-foot, ebony Baldwin grand piano. I am not a skilled musician and I am far from proficient at the keyboard. But the piano had been a sweet and loyal companion during the stormy passages of my youth. Because of my ADHD, the concepts of motivation and discipline were foreign to me. I never practiced scales. I never made it through instructional books that taught the classical style. And I never practiced what my teacher had assigned me to rehearse between lessons, unless my mother laid the belt on the piano and started the timer. Even then, I was a study in passive aggressiveness and could do so little with thirty minutes that it was hard to imagine. My mom, in exasperation, would threaten from the kitchen.

"David, you'd better get busy. Don't make me come in there and light a fire on your behind!" By far the worst punishment, though, was when I miscalculated her stores of patience and she would come in when there were only two minutes left on the timer and set it back to the beginning and make me start all over again. Ugh! Boring, boring, boring.

Then, around my sixteenth birthday, my parents finally realized that they were throwing away good money and released me forever from music lessons.

I happily put away all of my books from ten wasted years of piano lessons. Few people have had more instruction with less to show for it than I did.

For several months I didn't play at all. But after a while, I found myself sitting down and pecking around on the keys.

Then one Saturday, in the clean, light air of an unusually cool morning in the summer of my seventeenth year, I was shuffling down Scott Street in downtown Wichita Falls and saw a beautiful black grand piano in the window of Max Kreutz House of Music. I slipped inside and found no one there but an elderly salesman reading the paper at the counter in the back.

I wandered up and down the aisles, past uprights and spinets, and then past the grands. Their lids were smartly lifted like a chorus line tipping their hats. They smelled of oil and wood and polish and leather.

I looked over at the salesman, who was absorbed in the sports page.

"Would it be okay if I played this piano for a minute, sir?" I asked.

He looked a little annoyed, but seeing no one else there, said, "Go ahead, kid, but keep it down."

I slid onto the leather stool in front of a massive instrument that bore the name Steinway & Sons. I positioned my curved fingers over the keys, wrists slightly low. I played a C octave with my left hand and at the same time played a C major chord with my right.

As I held that chord, the sound that rolled out from the cabinet was sublime, delicious, and complex. It was the perfect pitch and tone to strike up a sympathetic vibration with my heart that reverberates to this day. From that seat on that Saturday, I could imagine that sound rolling down the hallowed halls and over the rows of seats and boxes of famed Carnegie Hall. I could imagine Mozart with his eyes closed, listening to my harmonies, with the same quickened pulse that I felt. Even now, I can hear that simple chord.

I slipped my right third finger down just slightly and struck the keys again, this time in a C minor chord. That tiny adjustment shifted sweetness and light to a darker, melancholic tone. This time when the piano spoke, it touched the place in me where pain and uncertainty reside, where the usually quiet tug of longing is suddenly keen, but with a confusing sweetness that I would not understand for many years.

That was all I played. I withdrew my hands and stared into the cabinet. I saw the copper-colored strings stretched tightly over the wood grain of the soundboard. It was orderly and perfect, a far cry from my haphazard interior.

Over the next few minutes, I browsed through the music books, passing quickly over the scores of instructional books and shelves stocked with classical music collections. Pausing to thumb through a few collections of jazz, I scratched my head in bewilderment at the crazy, convoluted scores. But when I came to Rock and Roll, I stopped abruptly, as if someone had called my name.

When I left the music store, I carried out my purchase, a single piece of sheet music. Before, the meager pay at my part-time job in the mall had always gone straight to buy food, in response to the insatiable demands of my teenaged, hyper-metabolizing body. That day, though, I bought an endless supply of nourishment for my fledgling soul in a piece of sheet music called "Time in a Bottle," by Jim Croce. Through thousands of music lessons and years of agony on the piano bench, I had been waiting for that music as surely as any penitent who has ever been converted by bread and wine. I had no idea what I had done, but looking back, I realize I carried home ambrosia for a buck fifty.

That night, I was thrilled to find I could play the song fairly easily, and I sang out Croce's haunting, heartbreaking, and eerily prescient lyrics with the confidence of a star. Alone at the keyboard, just a boy, a piano, and a song, a world opened up to me that I have explored ever since with enthusiasm and expectation. Books of music began to pour into my home as fast as my allowance and the job would permit. The music of Elton John, Billy Joel, Leon Russell, Carole King, Billy Preston, and Stevie Wonder became my passion and that raucous odd lot of artists became my heroes. Well past bedtime, when my folks and siblings were all in bed, I would ride the soft pedal and play long into the night.

I wish I could say a great talent was born of those nights, but the fact is that I still am only a mediocre player, at best. However, I hold the piano and those who have mastered her in a special place of respect and admiration. I see the instrument as an incarnation, God in instrumental form.

Since that breakthrough years ago, my love for the piano, like all true loves, has broadened and deepened. I still love the rock and pop keyboard artists who were the heroes of my youth. I also love the jazz piano of Diana Krall and Harry Connick, Jr, and in recent years, I have even overcome my early and persistent aversion to classical music. I have always appreciated the technical proficiency required to play classical music, but a real appreciation and enjoyment of the form had eluded me.

Recently, however, I have come to especially enjoy one particular type of classical music, the piano concerto. A concerto is a composition consisting of three movements written for a solo instrument along with an accompanying orchestra. While any instrument may be featured, concertos are most often written for piano. Mozart, Beethoven, Chopin, and Brahms are among the great composers who have been moved to create in this particular form. Sometimes the concerto is constructed in a way that highlights dramatic tension between the piano and the orchestra. Other concertos may be conceived as a collaboration and blend of the piano and orchestra.

The concerto is an apt metaphor for the process of psychotherapy. Sometimes the beauty and truth of the process are revealed in tension between the patient and therapist, and at other times it is expressed in the harmony and mutual resonance of the two.

The concerto is an apt metaphor for the process of psychotherapy. Sometimes the beauty and truth of the process are revealed in tension between the patient and therapist, and at other times it is expressed in the harmony and mutual resonance of the two.

In my practice, I have had the privilege of working with people who have been highly skilled artists of the piano. That work has been especially meaningful for me in part because I admire the instrument and those who play it well. And also because the problems that brought them into treatment, while not always directly related to the piano, were always affected and influenced by their relationship to the instrument.

I will never be skilled enough to play a concerto at the piano. I will leave that for those blessed with the talent and dedication to do so. But in the pages that follow I offer a literary composition called *Concerto for Piano*, written in three movements, and inspired by three amazing people, each an accomplished pianist, whose heroic struggles in life I have been privileged to hear and whose journey to healing I have had the great joy to witness. As you will see, they share a love of the instrument, but that love is manifest in very different ways, like different suitors obsessed in their own way with the same beloved. These stories, like musical compositions, are rendered in solitude, but subsequently shared openly with you, the audience.

While these three people and their stories are varied and unique, there is a common struggle and a common enemy shared by them. All of them were stuck in a shame that prevented them from experiencing themselves and their lives positively. As each movement unfolds, you will witness how the three courageously confronted the bondage of shame and found their way to new places after they drove it out of their lives.

As I write these stories, I am listening to the great concertos. Today, Mozart's Concerto Number 20 in C Major for piano and orchestra, the favorite concerto of the third pianist discussed below, plays to my inspiration and delight.

chapter seven

MOVEMENT ONE: IN THE SHADOW OF VAN CLIBURN

*What do you regard as most
humane? To spare someone shame.*
—Friedrich Nietzsche

HARVEL LAVAN "Van" Cliburn, Jr. was a child prodigy who began to play piano at three years of age. In 1958, at the height of the Cold War, the young American was invited to the Soviet Union's International Tchaikovsky Competition. The event was designed to highlight the superiority of Russian musicians, but when the slender 24-year-old played in the finals, he was given an eight-minute standing ovation. The legend in circulation about those events says that the judges were obliged to ask the Soviet Premier, Nikita Khrushchev, for permission to give the prize to the American. "Is he the best?" the premier asked. "Then give it to him!" Upon returning to the United States, Van Cliburn was celebrated with a ticker tape parade in lower Manhattan's Canyon of Heroes, the only such parade ever given to a classical musician.

Since the Van Cliburn Foundation inaugurated the Cliburn competition in Fort Worth, Texas, in 1962, its ascendency has been meteoric. Held once every four years, only a handful of the many thousands of gifted pianists is selected to participate. It is a pressure-packed event. To be chosen is an extraordinary privilege and honor. To win is the launching of an international career.

No doubt there are great stories to be told about the winners of that august competition. The aroma of fame and fortune is intoxicating, but loss is more complex and more intricate. The story that follows of one young man and how a singular aspiration came first to define, and then to break him, resonates in a dark, brooding, minor key. But while the anthem written in a bright, major key can stir us, it is only at the end of dissonance that we are absorbed by the sweet relief of resolution. And it is the resolution born of lost dreams and despair that communicates that most elusive and beautiful of human possessions—hope.

> *it is only at the end of dissonance that we are absorbed by the sweet relief of resolution.*

Josh and his piano had been divorced for twenty years. When their relationship had ended, what had once been a fulfilling life shared with his beloved was now an existence shared with bitterness, disappointment and shame, the cohabitants of a far more sterile world. The piano had been his love. For devotion to that instrument, he had forsaken all others, sacrificing the precious and sacred rites of youth. Friendships were forsaken which, for the boy in his teens, would have provided an antidote to the burden of parental expectations. Rebelliousness, another springboard to adulthood, was unimaginable for him. Perhaps most damaging of all, his blind infatuation with his piano never allowed him to access his whimsy, the hallmark and salvation of the young.

Across from me on the couch in our first session, he was a handsome man of 40, although he looked younger, almost boyish. He was dressed in a pressed white shirt worn tail-out, with jeans and loafers. Reddish hair was close-cropped and neat. His blue eyes were alternately smiling, imploring, and furtive. Eye contact was fleeting, but when he did look into my eyes, he seemed to be searching for something in particular.

In the first session, Josh described his struggle. Anxiety had folded him up smaller and smaller until there was little left of his life. He rarely left his apartment. Even stopping off at a fast food restaurant was a crisis. He felt like everyone was looking at him and judging him. His tiny apartment had become both his sanctuary and his prison. Of note, he had shut himself up without a piano.

At his birth, Josh joined a family that shared two legacies: music and melancholia. Josh was the youngest of five siblings, each with expressed musical interest and skill in some fashion. Josh's great-grandmother was a concert pianist. His mother played both the clarinet and the ukulele. She had played first chair clarinet in high school and had gone to college on a music scholarship. Josh's father and aunt both took lessons from Van Cliburn's mother. Josh's father liked the piano, but preferred playing basketball with Van while his sister was in her lesson. Van would grow to a Texas-size six feet and four inches, but according to the family lore, Josh's dad was the only friend who was allowed to play basketball with him. Apparently, Van's mother, already knowing how precious Van's gifted hands were, was certain that Josh's dad would not play aggressively with her son. So while Josh's father had the memories of playing basketball with one of the world's greatest musicians, Josh's aunt scored another legacy, being trained in piano by the mother and teacher of the great prodigy. His aunt went on to play the organ in church for the next 35 years.

Melancholia was a darker and more destructive endowment that marked this gifted family. Josh's great-grandmother, the concert pianist, gave up traveling around the South giving recitals to marry and have nine children. Along the way, something happened to her. She stopped playing and never touched the instrument again. She descended into depression and was committed to the Wichita Falls State Hospital, where she lived out the rest of her life. Her husband came to visit her faithfully until he succumbed to despair and committed suicide.

So often, it seems the great gift of creative genius and artistic abilities is coupled with, or perhaps born out of, the crucible of pain. William Blake, Jack London, Virginia Woolf, and Ernest Hemingway are among the writers and poets who struggled with mental illness. Van Gogh and Munch seemed to paint out of their mania. And musically, the list of those who, at some point, wrestled with mental illness stretches from Mozart to Schubert, from Hendrix to Clapton. It was to this fraternity, at once anointed and cursed, that Josh was destined to belong.

Josh began to exhibit an obsession with the piano from about three years of age. He was constantly touching it and playing on it even then. His family did not particularly recognize his gift until he was in third grade, when his first piano teacher went to his parents and impressed upon them just how gifted she thought he was. Shortly after, friends visiting the family home heard piano playing emanating from the music room. They remarked how much Josh's sister, a senior in high school at the time, had improved in her playing. To their considerable surprise, they were told by Josh's parents that the music from the piano was being played by eight-year-old Josh.

As time passed and his study of the instrument proceeded, the process became more and more central to his view of himself. In addition to the simple joy of playing, the piano offered him two comforts. He gained security in his competence, knowing that even if he was unsure and tentative in many ways, he was excellent in at least this one thing. The other, more dubious gift was the approval and praise he craved from other people.

His parents finally realized that Josh was one of the rarest and most remarkable of children, a prodigy. They determined they would give him all the support they could offer to see him fulfill the promise they believed was his destiny.

Unfortunately, they did not see that they had forsaken their own paths to significance. Consequently, their investment in his skills, although driven by love, was experienced by Josh as laden with implied expectations. They also did not understand that Josh's prolific skills at the piano were matched by an equal endowment of anxiety. His hands would flow up and down the keyboard with precision, speed, and grace, but his mind would be torturing him. His fear of failure and rejection lived in a terrible cycle with his growing musical competence. The more he achieved in his growth as a musician, the higher the stakes and the fear of failure.

Josh knew this instinctively. As time went by, he sensed that something was wrong, that while he worshipped the piano with all of his heart, he also lacked the joy he felt should accompany his accomplishments. He could enter into a musical piece and be wholly absorbed by it for a time, but lurking in the shadows was always a belief that he was a fraud and that very soon he would be exposed in humiliation and disgrace. It was only a matter of time. Not only would he be ruined by that failure, but his parents as well, by their hope and investment in him. Josh bore the burden of their unfulfilled dreams, and he could neither bear nor escape the thought of it.

As if this burden were not enough, an especially weighty, imagined expectation was felt by Josh like an anvil on his heart. Van Cliburn, his father's old basketball buddy, the lanky, laconic young man who had struck a heroic note in the Cold War, cast a gigantic, mythic shadow over Josh's sense of identity.

A narrative was then self-created, written on Josh's soul, that destiny had dictated that he say "yes" to his gift and excel at the piano. He would then rise among the ranks of lesser artists and ultimately fulfill his destiny at the Cliburn Competition. He could not slip or falter. He had to win at every level to maintain a trajectory that might someday lead to Fort Worth, fame, and fulfillment.

By rule of the event, the ages of the competitors are between eighteen and thirty. Therefore, calculating the years that competition would take place, Josh would have only two opportunities to compete before time slammed the door shut.

At first, the narrative played out as written. Josh won competition after competition and was soon playing with visiting artists in the Master Classes at Midland College. Judges, when awarding him a prize, seemed to go out of their way to praise his playing as if they were witnessing history being made. He earned top awards at the Piano Guild and the National Federation of Music Clubs. Stories about Josh's talent and promise appeared repeatedly on the front pages of area newspapers.

The next step was logical but would prove disastrous. Given the trajectory of his piano accomplishments to date, he would need a teacher who had the skill and commitment to catapult Josh beyond the throngs who aspired to the same illustrious goal.

After exhaustive searching, a woman of considerable reputation was selected as Josh's instructor. Maxine came highly recommended and had a long and impressive resume, a serious teacher for the serious student.

There are intersections in life over the horizon we can't yet see. If we could, we would stop or divert or do anything to avoid the misfortunes that lie ahead. These intersections are often benignly entered by decisions that seem unimportant or logical at the time. Had Josh or his parents been prescient enough to foresee what was ahead, they would have surely chosen differently. They thought by hiring Maxine, they were doing their utmost to promote their son's calling. But with that fateful choice, Josh began his forced march through youth that would end in the demise of his career and the shattering of his tender ego. The consequence of Maxine's employment was the onset of Josh's separation and ultimate alienation from the piano he had loved, and the music that had enlivened and inspired him.

> *There are intersections in life over the horizon we can't yet see. If we could, we would stop or divert or do anything to avoid the misfortunes that lie ahead.*

The nightmare that Josh survived in that relationship was inexpressibly difficult. Whereas his expectations for himself were already an extraordinary burden to bear, the expectations of his new teacher took the form of a monomaniacal control. That control reached far beyond piano. How much and how often he would practice was her domain, but she would also tell him when and how much to sleep and what to eat. She stood sentry on his contact with everyone, denying him the opportunity to make and maintain friendships. If he was ill, she became the doctor who would decide if, and when, he could go for medical care. She set impossible goals for him and then berated him when he failed, accusing him of "not wanting it badly enough." By far the most damaging strategy was what Josh referred to as the enigmatic "something else."

"She would sit me down, and instead of her usual stern countenance, she would soften just a bit, and then she would say, 'Josh, you are a fine musician. You might even be great. But if you give me what I am looking for, I will give you *something else*—something I have never given before. But it is something only I have the power to give you.'

"What do you mean by '*something else?*'" he would ask.

"I can't explain it. You have to figure it out. But when I listened to your performance, I didn't hear what I am looking for. You will never amount to anything as a musician unless you can find that quality I am looking for."

"Well, how will I know when I get it?" Josh asked.

"I will know. And I will tell you," she said.

"What do I need to do to get it?"

"Do everything I ask you to do," she said stiffly.

"I already do everything you ask me to do," he said.

"Obviously, you don't," she said, "because I don't hear it."

And so it would go on. Josh lived under an expectation that had no definition. He didn't know how to meet the expectation, except through abiding, unflinching and unquestioning allegiance to his teacher. He was led to believe that his future as a musician and his value as a person were measured by this inscrutable "*something else.*"

Her brutal reign lasted nine years, a little less than a decade but spanning his life from the pivotal ages of nine to eighteen. By the time Josh went to college and ended her tenure as his teacher, Maxine's malignant influence had thoroughly insinuated itself into his soul. Though he had attempted to quit Maxine three times, she always managed to lure him back. Even after he had escaped her direct manipulation, she still haunted him, bleeding off his joy.

One of the ways Maxine had consolidated her power over him was to win his mother's loyalty. Months after Josh had gone off to college and had been accepted as a student by a teacher considered to be one of the best in the world, Maxine appeared at Josh's family home. She had been through a surgery for cancer, and no sooner had she shown up than Josh's mother was taking her in to nurse her through her convalescence. By that time, Josh's fear of Maxine had given way to a simmering rage, and he refused to let her hear even one note of his playing. He suspended his piano practices the entire time she was in the house.

By all appearances, Josh's next teacher also saw his remarkable talent. Relieved to be free of Maxine's relentless tyranny, Josh hoped that he would now be able to fulfill his Van Cliburn dream with the help of a different mentor. Sadly, Josh's view of himself and the world had now been severely distorted. He was so fragile that not much was needed to break down his tenuous hold on reality and break open the stores of madness, the product of both Maxine's school of shame and his family's legacy of depression.

One day, after a few months of fairly promising work, the final act commenced without announcement or warning. Josh's teacher, after listening to a piece, remarked, "Josh, you will never do anything else."

In hindsight, what the tutor likely meant was that he saw Josh as destined to be one of the fortunate few musicians who were skilled enough to make a career of playing the piano. He was extending a highest compliment.

Sadly, when Josh passed that remark through the dark filter of his past, he heard, "Josh, you'd better be able to make the piano lucrative, because you are not good enough to do anything else."

Josh broke down on the spot, losing control of his emotions and weeping bitterly.

"Maybe you should get some therapy," his teacher helplessly suggested. But that suggestion only caused Josh to founder more. Wave after wave of shame rolled over him. He had been exposed as the impostor he had always known himself to be. His inevitable steep descent into brokenness and failure had begun.

Now, twenty years later, he was still spending his days and nights alone, emotionally barricaded in his small, government-subsidized apartment, without a piano or a passion.

"Josh," I began our session, "it is not all that uncommon for people who struggle with anxiety to find themselves home-bound. Tell me about your experience. Where do you think all this comes from?"

Instead of answering, he began fishing in his shirt pocket, withdrew a single photograph, and handed it to me. As I examined it, I could tell it was a picture of Josh, but barely. Some trauma had left him almost unrecognizable. With his right eye swollen shut, he stared from a left eye ringed by blood. Bruises discolored his face. Several lacerations appeared jagged and fresh.

"My God, Josh, what happened to you?" I asked.

"I had my car vandalized. Someone painted graffiti all over it. The same day I had picked it up from being repainted, three guys jumped me coming out of my apartment. I don't remember much about it really. I either lost consciousness or I blocked it out or something. I just remember coming around face down in the parking lot with blood all over me. Somebody saw me and called 911. The paramedics came and said I needed to go to the hospital. I didn't want to. I knew everybody at the ER and I didn't want them to see me like that, but I was hurt too badly to take care of myself, so I had to go."

"Josh, that must have been horrible. I am so sorry." I said. "Did they catch the guys who did this to you?"

"No, I know who did it, but I didn't press charges," He said. "That would only make it worse. I just holed up in my apartment and I've been waiting it out ever since."

Josh believed that in the small town where he lived, there were people who meant him harm. Because he didn't know everybody who might be involved, and because his memory of being assaulted reminded him of the consequences of venturing out, he chose to simply stay home. Being sheltered inside made him feel safe for the moment, but it also meant he would have to live as a recluse, cutting off ties to people and isolating himself from the things and interactions that make life worth living.

Looking back upon that session, I wish I had asked Josh *What was spray-painted on your car?* In psychotherapy, there are countless directions one can go in during any given session. You do your best to explore by asking good questions, but do not always come up with the exact one you should have posed. Inevitably, from time to time,

> In psychotherapy, there are countless directions one can go in during any given session.

you simply miss a question that might have gone to the heart of the matter, in this case, the heart of Josh's struggle with shame.

Unfortunately, I failed to ask that question for an entire year. In the first year of our work together, Josh made good strides on some levels. He was coming out of his apartment much more. He was becoming more assertive with the other people in his apartment complex who had often taken advantage of his passiveness and borrowed money he couldn't spare, but which they would never repay. He had begun talking about getting out of the town he lived in that had come to symbolize his shame. However, moving posed a problem because he was the only one available to take care of his aging parents, who lived in the same town. He felt stuck.

"If I could just get out of this town, things might be different," he told me.

In spite of his improvements, something was still missing. His steadfast avoidance of the piano, the object he had once considered essential to whom he was, concerned me.

"Josh," I said one session. "One of the things that makes me sad is that I have never heard you play. It feels difficult to know you, who you really are, without experiencing that."

"Doc, I do wish you could have heard me play. In contrast to all of the ways I am screwed up, I could do that one thing pretty well. Some days, the idea of playing again sort of sneaks up on me. But then, the pain and grief wash over me, and I shut it off. I just can't handle it."

So, week after week, the progress I hoped for him, evident in incipient form, seemed weak and superficial. Something was clearly missing. He followed my recommendation to undergo psychological testing, but the results were largely unrevealing. I already knew that he was depressed and suffered from chronic, pervasive anxiety. I knew he was passive and avoidant in his interpersonal relationships. But what was it? Why couldn't we get more momentum?

In psychotherapy, we talk often about the breakthrough. Sometimes, a patient's resistance is broken through. Sometimes, pent up or denied emotions spew forth in a relieving and cleansing flood. Sometimes, in a flash of insight, an illuminating answer emerges to shed light on some tenacious mystery. But the breakthrough moment in Josh's therapy was different, because it didn't happen to Josh, it happened to me. Josh wasn't even present.

The breakthrough came when I was preparing the psychological testing report. I was reviewing his records from Wichita Falls State Hospital, where he had been a patient eight years earlier. He had arrived in an apparently psychotic, rambling, disheveled, and paranoid state. In the record of his treatment, I finally learned the "word" that was at the heart of his shame. He had never uttered or even alluded to it in our year of therapy.

The chilling, ugly word was "fag." The shocking and heartbreaking fact was that the loathsome word was not just a point of fact in the hospital record. In his pain and self-loathing, Josh had actually taken a knife and carved the word on his own stomach. "Fag" had also been the word written on his car by vandals.

Scrawled in bright red paint across the side of it, and thereby tattooed on his soul, was the word that named his deepest shame. When I read it, I was angry with myself that I had missed it.

Homosexuality, in some parts of our culture, has moved beyond much of the prejudice with which it has been regarded in the past. Many sit-coms and movies routinely depict gay characters, although often in caricature. In the mid 70's, the American Psychological Association and the American Psychiatric Association removed homosexuality from the list of mental disorders.

Martin Luther King, Jr., once said, "The arc of history bends toward justice." As recently as the middle of the last century, the idea that people who were non-white would share the same rights and status as the dominant white culture was the cause of enormous social foment. Today, the idea is so mainstream that it seems a given. While covert racism remains a challenge to the world, racial equality has become a widespread belief, and to defend it is virtuous.

In the not too distant future, the same mainstreaming will undoubtedly occur around notions and beliefs about homosexuality. Justice will fall ripe from the vine of history, and if not we, our children will look back on our culturally, theologically, and legally sanctioned oppression of gay people as a

> *Changing social, cultural, and ethnic prejudices is a hard process.*

dark and regrettable reminder of our tendency to find people who are at all different as dangerous, misguided, or sinful.

But changing social, cultural, and ethnic prejudices is a hard process. Such change travels slowly, especially in parts of North Texas. Here, many young people who are gay still live in fear and shame. The vast majority of kids in school will not make it through the day without referring to something or someone they seek to ridicule as "gay."

The conservative, evangelical, Christian upbringing I mentioned earlier had pounded me in my youth about the "evils" of homosexuality. But somehow, I never bought into the fear-mongering. My closest friend, at 16-years-old, was asked to leave the church he loved because he was gay. I've been deeply wounded and angry about the church's decidedly unchristian approach to homosexuality. The first couple I treated as a psychologist-in-training at the University of

Louisville were two loving men, committed to each other completely, but each struggling with the life-long legacy of shame unrelentingly stuffed into them.

For the past twenty years, I have been the contracted psychologist to the Early Intervention Program in Wichita Falls, a program of the city Department of Health serving people who are HIV positive or have AIDS, many of whom are homosexual. As I have struggled and laughed and cried with gay men and women, I have tried to enter into their experience as much as I can as a heterosexual person. If there is a heaven, and if someone makes a mistake and offers me a spot, and if I find a sign on those pearly gates that says, "no gays allowed," someone else can have my ticket. If Nick and Kerry and Ellen and Ralph and a host of others are not able to get there on those grounds, it could never for one moment, let alone all eternity, be Heaven for me.

Given my passion for this critical issue, I could not believe I had missed it with Josh. I had erroneously assumed that he was not in a relationship with anyone because of his self-imposed cloister. There were factors, several of which I have described above, that I thought accounted for his intransigent shame, but this belated revelation cast a different light on everything.

"No wonder you were hiding out, Josh," I said. "They really were out to get you."

"Yeah, I have got to get out of that town," he said.

"Josh, we have been working together for over a year now. Yet, you never before mentioned that you were gay."

"I didn't think it mattered," he responded. In his characteristically self-deprecating style, he added, "Nobody would ever want me anyway."

Over the next few weeks, we talked at considerable length about his homosexuality. There wasn't anything in particular I said that significantly helped him accept the man he was, including his sexual orientation. This is one of the ways in which the relationship heals in psychotherapy. We met together each week, and instead of being buried in shame, his homosexuality was out in the open, along with the other parts of his life, both proud and problematic.

At the beginning of our work together, just coming to the office had scared Josh to death. Two years later, Josh and I had managed to create a much deeper, more honest relationship.

"I knew I was screwed up," he said, reflecting on those first sessions. "Coming in here, I realized that I needed to tell you all of my story. But I was so ashamed, I couldn't imagine how I could say those things about myself."

"What were the toughest things for you to say out loud?" I asked.

Josh thought about it for a minute. "Two things, really. There are people who know I am gay, but for some reason I dread talking about it. Still, I don't know why I waited so long to tell you. Actually, as I recall, I wasn't even the one who told on myself. It was my medical records that spilled the beans."

"I think you're right," I said with a smile. "And what is the second thing?"

"The other issue that was hard to discuss was about the piano. I had fallen so far. At twenty, I was somebody. People admired and respected me, even though down deep, I knew it was an act. When I came in here the first time, I felt like I was nothing. Living on disability, holed up in a crappy, subsidized apartment, just another loser. But not just another loser, I was a spectacular loser because of where I had fallen from. So many people around me have never had an opportunity. Life had never presented them with a real option. But me, I had a real talent, and the piano was my chance, and I failed."

"But not just another loser, I was a spectacular loser because of where I had fallen from. So many people around me have never had an opportunity. Life had never presented them with a real option. But me, I had a real talent, and the piano was my chance, and I failed."

"So what was it like to tell on yourself, to finally say it all out loud in this room?"

"Well, like I said, it scared me to death. But once it was out there, and you were listening and still smiling, I figured it was okay. At first, I wondered what you were going to think when I told the parts I was so ashamed of. I thought you were going to be disgusted, or that you were going to pity me or something. By the way, why *were* you smiling?"

"Josh, honestly, I wasn't aware I was smiling," I said. "But now that I think about it, I was smiling because I could see what was happening. You were showing courage. You were speaking the truth about yourself. You were not hiding from it anymore. And when that happened I knew you were about to meet the Josh I have known a long time, but has been a stranger to you."

"What are you talking about?" he asked.

"Well, from the first day you came in here, I could see you were burdened down by a ton of things. I didn't know what they were yet, but you were almost literally bent down under the weight of it all. It was like you carried this mantle of shame that made it impossible for you to stand up straight and see who you really were.

"So when you began to tell on yourself, I couldn't help smiling, because I could see you were about to shrug. I knew if you shrugged off all that shame, the Josh I could see, the intelligent, generous, inquisitive boy that was lost to you so long ago could come out to meet you. It was like I was watching a movie and when the climax of the plot came, I could see the ending was going to be really good, and I couldn't help smiling because I could see it all from that very moment."

"Well, I will admit that since I talked about it all and laid it out here, I have felt better," he said.

"Josh, I agree. You are making great progress. You are enrolled in school. You are talking about moving out of your hometown. You are getting out and going places and doing things. All of those things are important signs that you are on the move, and you are taking charge of your life again."

"It does feel good," he said.

"Well, a question occurs to me, given all you have accomplished. How are you feeling these days about the fact that you have not played the piano in close to twenty years?"

"Actually, I have thought about it more recently, but it still scares me. I mean, what's the point? I am way too old for the Cliburn Competition. I can't play in church because, being gay, I feel like a hypocrite."

For the moment, I left alone his statement about playing in church. I felt the time was right to make a little confession of my own.

"Josh, I have mentioned before that I took piano as a boy and that I am not much of a musician. In fact, I am terribly anxious about playing in front of anyone. My anxiety seems to come right out through my hands and I fumble all over the place. But I haven't told you how I came to love the instrument in my own way."

I told Josh the story about my first touch of a Steinway grand at sixteen years of age and my halting attempts through the years to play better. He listened with a relaxed smile of his own, and he seemed to be in step with me as I described the ecstasy of those C major and C minor chords. And finally, I told him about my piano.

"I have a six foot grand at my house. It was my graduation present to myself. It's no Steinway, but to me, it's beautiful. It has a lovely tone. I play only for me, but I find it healing and calming."

When he expressed approval, I asked him if he would like to play it.

Josh was surprised and a little stunned by my blunt invitation.

"I know it sounds a little odd," I said. "But clients and their therapists sometimes make an excursion outside the walls of the therapy office, as long as it is for an expressly therapeutic objective, and as long as it cannot be accomplished in any other way. Like a guy with a fear of elevators. They can talk about it in the office, but getting on an elevator in real life with the therapist along might help make that big step more likely. And for you, this may be a high yield opportunity. You have not played the piano in twenty years. I just can't see you living out the rest of your life without the piano. We could meet for our next session at my house. My family will not be there. If you feel up to playing something, that would be great."

I was not ready for this little turn of events. My own anxiety began to whirl at the very idea. Instinctively, and with more than a little cowardice, I ducked behind the therapist role.

Josh sat silently when I had finished pitching this rather unorthodox idea. I feared maybe I had been too abrupt and that he would feel I was pressuring him. His answer turned the exercise into a challenge for both of us.

"I will, under one condition," he said, "that you play something first."

I was not ready for this little turn of events. My own anxiety began to whirl at the very idea. Instinctively, and with more than a little cowardice, I ducked behind the therapist role.

"Josh, this is really not about me," I said. "It is about you and your relationship with the piano."

"I know that," he answered. "But you said you were anxious about playing in front of anyone else. I haven't touched a piano in two decades. It would probably help me if you played something first."

Then, with a smile, he added, "In fact, it would probably help if you could mess up a little."

"Oh, I am sure I could manage that, if nothing else," I said.

With that, we both agreed to this lively experiment.

The following week, I waited for Josh at my house. I raised the lid on the piano, and selected the piece I would play. I chose *Fools Rush In (where angels fear to tread)*, a favorite tune by Johnny Mercer that I had played countless times. In spite of that, I knew I couldn't possibly play it without lots of mistakes. I had not been groomed for this moment in my graduate school training.

Josh rolled up in his small pick-up truck at the appointed time. I met him at the door, and we exchanged nervous smiles.

"Well, here we are," I said. "Come on in."

We sat for a few minutes in the chairs that face the piano, and talked about how we both felt. We agreed; we each were nervous.

"It is a beautiful piano," Josh remarked.

"Thank you. I think so too," I replied. "How does it feel to imagine playing in a few minutes?"

"Doc, I've been thinking all week about this moment, and of course, I am anxious. But I have really been surprised by a feeling of excitement about doing this. I have really come to believe it is time."

"What are you going to play?" I asked.

"The piece I brought is called *Prelude, Chorale, and Fugue,* by Cesar Frank," he said. Then, breaking into a smile, he added, "But I think your turn is first."

My hands were already shaking when I sat down on the stool and arranged the music. Josh sat in the chair behind me. I took a deep breath. *Okay, let's do this.*

The first few notes were tentative, but the piano, as always, responded, and as the melody began to flow, I settled into the song. As expected, I made several mistakes, and at one point had to pause for a second to regain the flow of the piece. But all in all, I played the song better than I had thought I would. I was greatly relieved when I finally struck the last chord. I held the sustain pedal for a few seconds while it rolled through the cabinet and out into the room.

I lifted my foot and the music stopped. For a moment, there was silence. Then from behind me, I heard Josh's voice.

"I really enjoyed that, Doc. Thank you."

I felt a little guilty that I was so pleased by Josh's simple expression of thanks. This was supposed to be about him, not about me. But, I have to admit, I still took pleasure in his praise and I was grateful for his generosity.

I didn't say anything, but I stood and gestured that the piano was now his. Josh moved to the piano and paused. It appeared he was not pausing out of resistance, but out of consideration, perhaps at what an important moment this was for him. Perhaps the pause was a bow of respect and regard to the instrument. Part adversary, part lover, this cabinet of wood and steel was an extension of himself. It represented both the dark and traumatic past that had tortured him, and also what had once been the hope and promise of a fulfilling life.

When he ended his silent tribute, he sat down. A ritual then played out as he adjusted the position of the stool and placed the music on the rack. Every movement was fluid, precise, and seemed to point to a higher purpose, like a devout priest folding away the veil and preparing the sacred elements of the mass. There was a deep respect in every movement as he spread the complex score out before him. In spite of whatever he might have been experiencing emotionally, there was no observable hint of hesitation or doubt.

My piano has been a loyal companion to me. When I play, my music sounds better than if I were playing on an inferior instrument. But through my endless hours of playing, I was aware that my piano was capable of far more than I could demand. I imagined if a piano could feel, mine must have been thrilled under Josh's gifted touch. It must have realized for the first time since the day it had been so lovingly fashioned, the true purpose for which it had been made.

A confluence of artistry rose up in my living room on that spring afternoon. The piano builder, the artisan whose skill and passion years before had selected and shaped raw components to craft the instrument, had provided the foundation. Upon that endowment, Cesar Frank had composed an exquisite musical potential. But before the sweet alchemy of music could take place, a gifted, musical magician must give it life. It required Josh to take the dream of the composer and to execute the ballet of movement that translated into the music that danced around me that day.

I sat transfixed, not only by the arresting beauty of the song, but by what I witnessed as Josh played. Instead of his fingers moving to strike the keys, they appeared to be lured to them by some inexorable force. The room filled as the piece rose in soaring crescendo. Josh leaned slightly forward, head down, his hands a blur. Then leaning back, he moved into a more contemplative passage, rich with delicate harmonies that explored the thematic variations of the fugue. I closed my eyes and let the sounds flow through me, sublime and serene at one point, then overwhelming and triumphant the next.

Two decades of pain and shame were transcended in that moment, like estranged lovers who found their separation dissolved in the healing elixir of reconciliation. All too soon, the piece was over. This time it was Josh who held down the sustain pedal, drawing out the last drop of sound as if reluctant for it to end.

When at last he gently lifted his foot, we sat in silence. Neither of us knew what to say, or perhaps we didn't need to say anything at all.

After a few moments, I broke the silence. "Well, what was that like?"

"It was a little rough in spots," he said.

I first smiled broadly and then broke into laughter. I wasn't surprised that Josh would take such a moment and manage to find fault with it. I was quite sure that critique didn't fully summarize his experience.

In response to my outburst, he smiled sheepishly and added, "Actually, that felt pretty good."

"I'll say. That was pretty good indeed, Josh. Thank you so much for sharing that with me."

Over the next few minutes, Josh and I processed his feelings about playing for the first time in twenty years. He said he had anticipated that it would take a long time to be able to actually enjoy playing again, if he ever could. But he said that he had sensed, almost from the first note, a deep satisfaction that could never have been predicted.

"I felt like I was coming home," he said.

Although playing that day had been a breakthrough for Josh, the experience did not entirely purge him of shame in his heart and life. We continued to work together over the next year. Some situations became tougher. His parents' health declined, making him forestall his plans to move out of the town that had been such a source of fear and anxiety to him. But he was getting out much more and with far less trepidation. He enrolled in a university about an hour away, where he especially enjoyed classes in psychology and philosophy.

Perhaps, the most important evidence that Josh had made an assertive move toward healing was twofold. First, with the help of his parents, he purchased an old grand piano. It needed a lot of work, and it was a far cry from the Steinway he had sold so long ago, but it was a piano, and it was his.

The other was that Josh, overcoming his usually passive style, made an appointment with the best piano teacher in the area, a professor at the university who was an accomplished concert performer. He dealt courageously with the pressure of auditioning for her. Upon hearing him play, she immediately offered to teach him. She also encouraged him to take on a major in piano performance, an option he said he would consider.

These days, when I sit at my piano and struggle to raise up my own simple musical offerings, I often recall the day when Josh walked out of that prison of his own making and went home to his true self, to his music, and to the piano. And I decide to stay and play a little longer.

chapter eight

Our revels now are ended. These our actors,
As I foretold you, were all spirits, and
Are melted into air, into thin air:
And like the baseless fabric of this vision,
The cloud-capped tow'rs, the gorgeous palaces,
The solemn temples, the great globe itself,
Yea, all which it inherit, shall dissolve,
And, like this insubstantial pageant faded,
Leave not a rack behind. We are such stuff
As dreams are made on; and our little life
Is rounded with a sleep.

The Tempest, Act 4, Scene 1

—WILLIAM SHAKESPEARE

MOVEMENT TWO: FROM INVISIBLE WOMAN TO IMAGO DEI

PROSPERO, THE PROUD father of the bride in William Shakespeare's *The Tempest*, descibes a world within a world—a picture of life that is similar to Russian nesting dolls.

Nesting dolls have delighted children for centuries. Inside each hand-painted and crafted doll sits a smaller replica. As the child discovers that her doll opens, she finds another inside the first until she comes at last to hold the tiny prototype that rests at the center of it all.

The philosopher and psychotherapist are like that child playing with the nesting dolls, only we start from the inside and try to find our way out of the narrow confines of our lives as they are first experienced and understood. When we break out of that confinement, we gain a new level of insight into ourselves and a new level of freedom. Socrates' admonition to "know thyself" refers to this process. Unlike the scientist who starts outside and works her way in deeper and deeper, reducing everything in search of the core elements, the philosopher seeks new levels of awareness that open and open to reveal who we truly are when we have been relieved of our mistaken perceptions.

Self-reflection is one of our primary tools to create meaning in our lives.

Human beings are blessed with the great gift of being able to step outside of our experience and direct our attention back to the way we were experiencing our lives just a moment ago. Our thinking can be like mirrors reflecting each other. We can think about ourselves thinking about ourselves thinking about ourselves.

Self-reflection is one of our primary tools to create meaning in our lives. Without it love, morality, faith, freedom, and friendship would have no meaning.

Mental illness is an impairment in the reflective self. The ability to step outside and redefine oneself from the new, truer perspective is impaired or

Mental illness is an impairment in the reflective self.

lost. Psychosis is essentially becoming locked in a certain perspective and being unable to relinquish it. The sufferer of delusion can't make use of evidence disconfirming the mistaken belief.

For those with depression, melancholia descends and the sufferer can't shake the sense that everything looks dark. Or a panic disorder maintains its ability to torture by a critical error in estimation that some dreaded event will occur. What actually has a remote chance of happening now seems inevitable.

In the daily life of the mentally ill, the image of life as nesting dolls is anything but pleasant. Instead, it belies a prison of many levels. The afflicted can't get out of their old patterns of feeling and behavior to see things in a different way, and there seems to be a virtually infinite number of levels of incarceration that stand between them and joy.

Sarah appeared to be serving a life sentence in her mental illness. The term "chronic mental illness" is no longer en vogue, replaced by "serious and prolonged mental illness." Sarah's level of demoralization and hopelessness was hard to overstate in any terms.

Sarah was referred to me after a psychiatric hospitalization. Her psychiatrist had treated her for a number of years, and I suspect that his suggestion that she see me in therapy was more out of desperation than confidence in me. She had been severely troubled for years and had tried about every known psychiatric drug, as well as various outpatient and inpatient therapies.

"I feel like I'm invisible," was her presenting complaint, which was accompanied in her demeanor by a melancholy expression and the flexion of her jaw muscles. Sarah's word "invisible" brought on a distracted moment. I knew that Sarah meant an "existential" invisibility, not a literal one, but the old joke by Henny Youngman still blindsided my focused, undistracted self. *The psychiatrist's secretary buzzes into his office: "Doctor, there is a man out here who needs an emergency session. He says he is invisible." The doctor replies, "Tell him I can't see him."*

However, when I am at my best, those random distractions are fleeting, and I recompose and try to move back into the moment.

Sarah went on to describe what she meant. "As I look back, I can't remember a time when I felt I mattered at all, that people took notice of me. Now I am completely isolated from everybody and everything. I am so angry I could explode."

As I listened, I sensed the depth of Sarah's isolation. I felt an almost tangible wall even between us. She registered the staggering stressors she had faced without inflection, almost as if she had covered this ground so many times that she did it by rote. The wall had obviously been composed, in part out of anger.

When she came to see me, she had recently lost her beloved husband. A surgery had left her with permanent nerve damage, leaving her with chronic pain and ending her career as an RN. She had essentially no income. The work she was doing on her Master's Degree was interrupted. And then, just when she needed emotional support, her late husband's family pulled back from her. Add to all of those immediate stressors, the long history of her struggle with depression and anxiety.

"I've been hospitalized over fifteen times. I have carved on myself. I've had six different courses of shock treatments. I've lost count of the number of times

I have attempted suicide. I've driven off a highway bridge at a hundred and ten miles an hour, and somehow didn't even get hurt. I have been diagnosed with almost everything at one time or another: Major Depression, Bipolar Disorder, Obsessive Compulsive Disorder, Borderline Personality Disorder, and ADHD. When I glimpsed at my chart last week at Red River Hospital, I saw written there two words that sum is all up—poor prognosis.'"

Sarah paused there and waited. I understood the pause. *What makes you think you can help me? No one can help me. I am way beyond help. What can you possibly do that I haven't already tried?*

What indeed? I thought. *What can I say? Where do I start?* Often with new patients, I have a pretty good idea about what might be a fruitful direction to begin our exploration by the end of the first session. But with Sarah, the wall between us was as substantial as it had been at the onset. I had no idea about how to begin bringing that wall down.

All I had to start with was a certain bias regarding Sarah. Most of the time, the diligent therapist seeks to identify and weed out bias whenever it occurs in the therapeutic relationship. But with Sarah, I was well aware of a bias, and I made no attempt to let it go. That bias related to her intrinsic value as a person. It is precisely her uniqueness, that was not even evident yet, that inclined me toward her, and drew me into relationship with her. So as I experienced that wall between us in the early going, my bias was that it obscured from me the uniqueness that would one day be revealed if we were both courageous enough to dismantle that barrier. I suspected that the wall was encountered by everyone else, too, and when they withdrew from, or were repelled by that wall, Sarah took it as a rejection, as a repudiation of her as a person.

I had been called to be loyal to the woman behind that wall. I had to believe, even if I could not see her, that we were alike.

So I endeavored to be faithful to the unique, wondrous person I believed was in there. I began this book with a quote by Bonhoeffer, where he refers to the "loyal heart" that can change the face of sorrow. In that tradition, I had been called to be loyal to the woman behind that wall. I had to believe, even if I could not see her, that we were alike. We both wanted to know who we were. We both wanted to be loved. We both wanted to know why we were here in this life. And we both had a nemesis in shame.

That is simply my bias. I am not sure where it comes from. My upbringing in the Judeo-Christian tradition undoubtedly played a part. Americans are also taught that each person has an inalienable right to pursue life as he or she chooses to live it. But even beyond those influences, I have come to believe in and to pledge allegiance to every new patient I meet, a unique, worthy individual sitting in front of me.

No matter what the substance or the size of that wall that stood between Sarah and

I have come to believe in and to pledge allegiance to every new patient I meet, a unique, worthy individual sitting in front of me.

me, I was committed to stay with the conversation until the barrier came down. I had no doubt about her precious, unique individuality. I had no idea, either, how long we would have to share a path together to find out. Perhaps I would have shrunk from the task had it not been for a glimpse here and there of what might be possible.

Thankfully, events sometimes happen in life that prefigure great things to come. My personal favorite was a moment shared with the beautiful mother of my children. As we were expecting each of our four babies, we would go to the doctor's office for a sonogram. We didn't get a snapshot of a smiling, blond-haired blue-eyed baby we would soon hold in our arms, rather a shadowy, grainy image. Peering intently at the little screen, one or the other of us would always say in wonder, "My God, did you see that?" In that fluid, slippery world was movement. I could see a little bowed head and two little arms, with hands stuffed in a little mouth. And perhaps most amazing, I could see a tiny beating heart. Our hopes and our dreams were being miraculously transformed into living flesh and blood right before our eyes. But for the time being, we would have to wait.

In our first session, Sarah gave me a message that prefigured what was to come for us. I heard the word "piano."

"Sarah, you have spoken of the things that have been problems for you in your relationships with others. You said how little you get from them. Actually, you said these relationships are one of the aspects of life that troubles you most. Could you give me an example from your life right now?"

"Yes, I can," she said. "I'm Catholic and I sometimes play the piano at my church. But lately, I have not felt like I am a part of the program, and I almost have to beg to get to play."

I was surprised when I heard she played piano, although I heard everything she said. I don't know why that struck me. Perhaps because she seemed so unhappy and unfulfilled, it was hard to believe she possessed a talent that, in my experience, was such a great gift. She was sitting on a gold mine. That she played piano was like a message from the other side of the wall.

"Let's talk about that for a minute," I said. "Tell me about you and the piano."

Sarah was transfigured by my invitation. Her eyes, downcast throughout the session, rose to meet mine. Her face became animated as she told me about her life with music and the piano.

Sarah's mother was a lover of music, especially piano. She introduced Sarah to it early on, and by the age of six, Sarah was already playing well with both hands. She blazed through the instructional books she was given, and by the time she was eight she was playing for the Women's Forum gatherings.

She stopped formal lessons at the age of twelve, but she didn't stop learning. She educated herself in a wide variety of musical forms. The eight-volume *Encyclopedia of Piano* was one of her great challenges, and she committed to work her way through it, beginning to end.

Those years in adolescence were fruitful, but required little of Sarah in terms of interpersonal interaction. Her lessons were "private" because she taught herself. She became quite accomplished, making it to the regionals in piano at North Texas State University. Upon entering college, she successfully auditioned to become a piano performance major.

Even though Sarah loved the piano, her relationship to the instrument was not without its complications. She never felt that her talent was enjoyed or esteemed by her family. Her father never came to a recital. Early on, her sister seemed jealous of her ability and her brothers made fun of her.

These rejections were difficult for Sarah to bear, but when she was alone at the piano, she was able to move them aside for a little while. When she played to the approval of others, she enjoyed rare moments when she felt that others really saw and recognized her. She was not invisible.

As Sarah recounted these memories of her piano performances, she often smiled. There was a fleeting lightness to her bearing and speech that offered a clue to her path out of depression and despair.

As soon as Sarah moved away from the subject of her beloved piano, the melancholia that dogged her day in and day out took hold again, pulling her down. I could only watch helplessly as she slipped back beneath the waves.

In this age of managed care, symptom-focused therapy, and evidence-based practices, the average length of psychotherapy is probably about eight sessions. Some people, like Sarah, need more time. She came to me for about five years, most of that time on a weekly basis. Had we not had such a liberal allotment of time, I am quite certain not much would have come of our work together. Our process was a marathon, but through it all Sarah showed a tenacity that surprised me, given the deep state of demoralization in which she began. Perhaps there was something in the nature of the connection we had formed that she found encouraging. Maybe she felt that this was her last hope, and it was desperation that held her in the work. Whatever it was, she stayed with it, and stayed with me until we were closing in on three hundred sessions together.

What do a therapist and a patient have to talk about for all those sessions? After a while, haven't most of the issues of interest been talked out? Sarah's therapy with me was characterized by three epochs. First, and most difficult, was the establishing of trust. Second was the epoch of sharing together her narrative, and third was the era of openness and progress.

Establishing trust was the most difficult, not because Sarah was suspicious of me, although I suppose she might have been in the beginning. She was respectful of me to a fault. Frequently, she would opine that she was wasting my time, better spent with someone for whom there was some hope for change and growth. I never knew if those statements were driven by self-deprecation or the need to hear me reaffirm that she was worthy of my time and that I was not bored or frustrated with her.

The problem with trust was her struggle in trusting in the process at all. She had been through so many and varied courses of treatment, she was finding it hard to have any faith that what we were doing could make any difference whatsoever.

Sarah thought she had exhausted all less invasive procedures, like psychotherapy, long ago. She had submitted to drug therapy and tried just about every psychoactive substance on the market. When those had proven ineffective, she had agreed to electro-convulsive therapy, perhaps the most invasive treatment around these days.

Far from arrogance about my own therapeutic abilities, I simply have deep respect for the human tendency toward growth and change. With remarkable frequency, I have seen people break free from the gravity of the past.

It seemed unlikely to her that psychotherapy held much promise after all she had been through and all she had tried. She must have thought I was presumptuous to believe we might succeed after many experienced therapists had given it their best effort and psychiatry had exhausted its entire bag of tricks to no avail. But as I have often said, "Fools go where angels fear to tread." Far from arrogance about my own therapeutic abilities, I simply have deep respect for the human tendency toward growth and change. I am not easily discouraged. With remarkable frequency, I have seen people break free from the gravity of the past.

Another issue in the process of psychotherapy is the chemistry between the therapist and patient. Sometimes the fit is just not right, and no matter the skill of the therapist or the commitment of the patient, the wheels just seem to spin, and progress remains elusive. Conversely, the therapist might be quite new to the process and the client might even be ambivalent about the need to change at all, and the outcome is nevertheless powerful and the change enduring.

Time and again, I have seen my own predictions about a patient's prognosis be completely wrong. Sometimes a patient comes in with what appears to me to be minor adjustment issues that should only take a few sessions to resolve, and yet therapy is later terminated in frustration and in the absence of any meaningful change. Then again I have been astounded by dramatic change I had never thought possible.

Over my years in practice, I have determined that my job is to stay faithful to the process. I have resolved to stay away from predicting outcomes. I try to stay optimistic about the possibility of change, even when the patient cannot.

The first agonizing epoch of my work with Sarah was characterized by grave doubts on her part and a dogged optimism on mine. I certainly had doubts, but I was called to act in spite of my doubts, which I guess is the definition of having faith.

For two years, Sarah told me tales of her sorrow and rejection. She had a huge chip on her shoulder over the way life had treated her. Every human interaction she encountered inevitably ended up reaffirming her unworthiness and invisibility. There appeared to be a destructive cycle powerfully maintaining her unhappiness. She felt unworthy and had come to expect others to reject her, so when she encountered a situation where she could reach out for support, she was loath to do so, fully expecting rejection. When she would finally muster enough courage to try to engage others, she approached the situations so tentatively and with such obvious suspicion that others undoubtedly sensed her trepidation. They would then react by distancing themselves from her out of their discomfort with her hesitant approach. So she would take it as another personal rejection, based not on her lack of social skill, but upon her basic lack of value as a person.

Again and again, she would ask in a dozen different ways, "Is there not one person who really sees me who is not going to reject me?"

I tried to verbally answer that question without pitying her. I did work with her many times on social skills. She would bring in an interpersonal failure she had experienced, and we would do the autopsy on the interaction, noting alternatives she might try. We would also reframe things she had said that came across as hostile or defensive.

But that basic question about her perceived invisibility remained unanswered. I was working in every way I knew how to respond affirmatively. I knew one person who was working very hard to see her, value her beauty, intelligence, and talents, and not reject her. That person was me.

In a wonderful story told in the Bible, Jesus was taken and tried before Pontius Pilate. The governor, thinking he might exploit the opportunity to test this man who many claimed to be a great teacher, asked Jesus, "What is the truth?"

The story says that Jesus just stood there. Of course, he was answering Pilate, although not with words, but with his presence. Jesus was saying, "You want to know the truth? Know me." His presence spoke far more than words could have.

In the process of psychotherapy, words seem to dominate. We do, after all, call it "talk therapy." But those who have made this process their life's work know very well that the best and most powerful moments are often not about the words. Rather, it is the shared time and shared space between two people who are joined in a common search for meaning and purpose. And though I never said it out loud, I think the first epoch of our work was successful because Sarah came to know by my faithful presence that I did really see her and that I would not reject her.

The second part of our work began after months of exploring the emotional pain Sarah faced every day. In the course of those many hours, she had often alluded to events in her life that had been especially troubling. Her first marriage was to a man for whom she held nothing but contempt. Her second marriage made her a widow. The miracle man she had married had joyously come into her life and encouraged her when she least expected it. Then he was tragically taken from her a few years later, consigning her once more to her prison of isolation and mental illness.

Beyond these events, I knew little of her family of origin, or what her youth had been like. We spent a few months exploring the varied terrain of her childhood. That experience was startling in its pains and joys. Conscious of the pain she had encountered in those days, Sarah was surprised by the power of other forgotten memories that made her smile and feel the warmth of nostalgia. She had not thought about many of those long ago events in a considerable time.

She recalled that she had, at times, delighted people when she played the piano. In those moments, the music took her through a passageway into peace, where the constant striving to shore up a faltering ego could be released to float along on the wings of the song, effortless and without fear.

She recalled the pride of going with her mother to pick out a new house. Sarah had been five, and she hadn't realized that she was only alone with her mother because the rest of the children were in school. It didn't matter. As far as she was concerned, her mother was consulting only with her about the beautiful two-story home she had raced through with abandon. It was her house. *She* had picked it out.

She managed a rare positive memory of her father, when he took the family out on the lake and taught Sarah and her siblings to water ski. She closed her eyes as she told me, and I could see that, for a moment, she was a girl again, with a rope in one hand, slipping through warm summer water as smooth as glass. Then, switching hands, she carved the ski through the water in a graceful arc, dipping her shoulder low to the surface, and finally shooting across the boat's wake, swinging far out to the opposite side, where it seemed she and the boat were in a race she could almost win.

"David, I haven't thought about those things in years. Why don't I recall those more often?"

"I'm not sure," I said, "but I think it probably has something to do with the way depression tends to obscure the good and beautiful things in life. It's really quite surprising. A few years ago, I went snow skiing with some friends, and they let me borrow a pair of goggles that had a yellow tint to them. I remember when I put them on I saw the whole world in that amber color. But as I skied that day, I noticed that very soon my eyes adjusted and no matter how

> *Depression changes our perspective in a way that many of the good things in life are obscured, like they never existed at all.*

hard I looked, I could not detect that yellow tint at all. Then at the day's end, I took the goggles off and to my surprise, everything looked blue.

"I think that's what depression does to us. It changes our perspective in a way that many of the good things in life are obscured, like they never existed at all. And when we are confronted unavoidably by good things we dismiss them and suspect they don't actually exist."

"I have been wearing those dark glasses so long," Sarah said in resignation. "It's just the way I see the world now."

"Well, Sarah," I said. "Let's take them off and see what we see then!"

Dubious, she looked at me. "Easier said than done, right?"

"Yes and no," I said. "" A moment ago, when you were telling me that great story about water-skiing, you had a smile on your face and you were almost transported back to the experience. Am I right?"

"Yes, I could really see it and feel the water and the sun and everything."

"So you can do it. You are capable. The hard part is to learn to do it all the time, to recognize when depression has lowered the veil. As a matter of fact, as you rehearse your narrative, I would like for you to practice this awareness. If the things you are recalling are painful, we will be fully open to the pain, but if it is sublime or exciting or sweet, we are going to be open to that also, okay?"

"I'll try," she said tentatively.

"Well, take me back now with you. Tell me what you remember from your family and your childhood."

With that invitation, we launched into the second epoch of our work. Sarah was raised in a family of some means, not wealthy, but well off. Her father, Jason, she recalled as a man shrouded in mystery. Almost everything she knew about him she learned through her mother. His passion was flying and he was a pilot for a major airline. His father-in-law bribed him into moving back to Texas to work in the oil business with the promise to buy him an airplane. Even though Sarah's father accepted the offer and moved the family back, the promise was never fulfilled. That didn't thwart Jason. He went on to buy and fly several airplanes on his own. In Sarah's estimation, he was a workaholic and an alcoholic (read "big drunk"). He appeared to work hard so that his family could enjoy good things, but there was never a hug, or a kiss, or a word of encouragement.

Sarah's mother, Ann, was a force of nature. She kept a diary from the age of twelve until she married at nineteen. Her father was a chauffeur and she suffered for that heartless teasing from the children she went to school with, many of whom were children of the wealthy and famous. After she married, she had four children, kept a spotless house, volunteered for several community service projects, and was one of the finest trap shooters around, traveling all over the country bringing home one trophy after another.

Eventually, they had that nice, two-story home, a cabin at Lake Texoma, and an airplane to go back and forth in. Although it sounded idyllic, it took a tragic turn when Sarah's father began an affair. Her mother was crushed.

She had never been a quitter in anything, but had not been challenged like this before. She took the children to the lake to get her bearings. After a few days, Jason came to the lake house, hat in hand, to try to reconcile with Ann. While there, Jason suffered a massive heart attack and died a few days later in the hospital at Sherman, Texas.

"I never understood why no one called me until the day he died. I never got to see him before he died."

Sarah had three capable and successful siblings. For a time, she shared a room with Shannon, the eldest. Sarah suspected that Shannon was probably "driven mad" by her little sister's anger and hypersensitivity. Her brothers, Jason and Greg, were the middle children. Sarah was especially close to Jason, and she was devastated when he died of cancer at fifty-two, nine months after her mother passed.

Sarah was present at her mother's death. She felt that she had died bitter, resentful still over her husband's unfaithfulness and death, and angry over her beloved son's cancer. In fact, she suspected that her mother had willed herself to die because she could not bear to outlive her son.

"So that's my family," Sarah said. "I only have Shannon and Greg left. They seem to prefer each other's company to mine, and that bothers me sometimes. They are both business types, but they are good people."

"That brings us to the point of the story when you reach adulthood," I said.

"Yeah," she said. "We are about to get to the part where the wheels really come off."

While working at her first job at Sam Gibb's Music, she met Donny, a "nerdy-looking," mustached boy. They dated briefly. He took her to meet his family in Dallas, and she was appalled at their shack of a home and the vile bigotry of Donny's father.

"But I didn't think I could be picky, so when he asked me to have sex with him, I just gave it up," she said.

"Why did you think you couldn't be 'picky' as you say?"

"Because I've never been pretty," was her matter-of-fact reply.

"I know this about myself," she said. "I was told over and over by the neighborhood boys. My dad bought my sister Shannon all kinds of beautiful clothes, and never once did so for me. I can still remember a woman who was a former stripper saying to me, 'You're not pretty, not cute, but you could be attractive *if* you tried.'"

As I listened to Sarah reel off the case against her appearance, I felt the pull to argue with her. She had shown me a family picture when she was in her 20's and by any estimation, she was an attractive woman. During the times we had met, she had often alluded to her so-called unattractiveness. She said men never paid attention to her. By her presentation, I was not surprised. She walked with her head down and a chip on her shoulder. Her countenance said, "Approach at your own peril." The lack of male attention had nothing to do with her physical appearance. Nevertheless, the myth of unattractiveness is hard to overcome, and the insecure person is always the last to be persuaded otherwise. The sad thing was that Sarah gave herself away first sexually and then in marriage because she thought she deserved no better. This self-defeating behavior would haunt her throughout her life.

The myth of unattractiveness is hard to overcome, and the insecure person is always the last to be persuaded otherwise.

When Donny proposed, she at first declined, but when he broke down crying and pleading, she had relented. Shortly afterwards, she gave birth to her only child, a little girl, Abby.

The marriage didn't last long. Sarah's fragile hope for a peaceful life for herself and her little girl would also end in a storm.

From Sarah's earliest memories, she had felt possessed by a capricious and malevolent spirit. Even as a little girl, she would instantly become a whirling dervish, a tiny wrecking-ball of rage with the slightest provocation. Her outbursts were so bewildering to her family that, at first they would stand back in amazement, and later would just retreat until the storm passed. The source of all of this fury was unknown to them, but as I listened to Sarah's recounting, I wished that someone had had the courage to risk wading into the rage and wrapping a pair of loving arms around this little girl and reminding her how precious she was. Instead, Sarah's family's action, standing by or retreating during these episodes, reinforced the notion that she was a freak, that she didn't belong, that she was, in fact, invisible.

I thought about that word *invisible*. In my early twenties, I was planning to enter the Christian ministry as an urban minister, working with poor people. Realizing I had spent my whole life as a middle-class white kid, I decided one night to dress up like a homeless person and spend the night on the streets. I went to the Good-Will store and found a pair of tattered pants and some shoes with about a hundred thousand miles on them. Over a dirty tee-shirt, I put a hideous suit jacket with the lining torn out. I found a ball cap that advertised a bait shop. The coup-de-grace was a cigar I bought, broke in half and burned off the end. I had never smoked anything with the exception of that joint I had tried when I was eighteen, but I had braces on my teeth and had to hide them. No one was going to buy the idea of a homeless guy with braces.

Walking down Lancaster Street toward downtown Fort Worth, Texas, I entered Braum's Ice Cream store for a drink of water. As I entered and walked to the back of the store where the water fountain was, I was struck by the oddest feeling. I was *invisible*. In normal life, I was at least regarded with a glance or a nod. Dressed as I was that night, not one person looked up when I entered. The staff at the restaurant didn't ask what I would like to order. Parents with children seated in booths turned ever-so-slightly toward their kids, as if to focus on them a little more. It was clear to me, however, that they were intentionally, or perhaps instinctively, declining to acknowledge my existence. So powerful was that experience that I shuddered to think what it would be like if my entire life were spent like that. Perhaps Sarah's fits were not so surprising after all.

The problem for Sarah was that the episodes became a self-fulfilling prophesy. She would feel so marginalized and invisible that she would react in rage and anger, which, in turn, would make people back up and pull away, which would confirm that she was not worthy of attention and connection, which would elicit rage, and the cycle would continue.

Mark Twain is credited with saying, "Some people would jump off the cliff today for fear of jumping off the cliff tomorrow." Sarah launched into adulthood as a young mother with a deep conviction that she was worthless, invisible, and willing to rage in order to overcome it. When her rages had consequences, this would only confirm what she already so unflinchingly believed.

Sarah quit her job at Sam Gibb's Music in a rage. She took a job at a finance company and left that job after she erupted in anger at the bigoted manager who was her boss. She got a job that she loved at a hospital, but she left after an outburst. When Abby was five, Sarah and Donny divorced. Sarah was awarded custody of Abby, but Donny took her anyway and kept her for two weeks. In an age before sanctions against people who kidnapped their own children were in effect, all Sarah could do was frantically beg him until he finally brought her home.

Sarah soon descended into depression and was hospitalized with her first "nervous breakdown." During her three months there, she received her first course of electro-convulsive therapy. Sarah had made arrangements with a family to care for Abby while she was away, but Donny snatched her while she was playing in the front yard. Weeks later, he was found hiding with her in Del Rio, Texas. Again, he let her come home.

The third time Donny took Abby, Sarah had exhausted her financial resources. A challenge for Abby's custody would have to be in Dallas County. She and Donny were battling by phone. Finally, Sarah agreed to leave Abby with Donny, as long as she could have her on weekends and summers.

The next few years were characterized by one attempt to move ahead after another, each undermined by another breakdown. At twenty-seven, Sarah went to college to study piano, but she had a panic attack when it came time to play a recital. She had never before been anxious about playing. Now, that source of peace was gone, too.

Sarah converted to Catholicism and moved in with some Catholic Sisters. Although the Sisters were apprehensive about her decision to go to nursing school, she went anyway. This was a time of both proud successes and frustrating failures. On a high note, she was the president of her nursing class. On a devastatingly low note, she became pregnant, but to her horror, she could not recall how. She wonders to this day if she was raped and has blocked out the memory. Her doctor insisted that she terminate the pregnancy and she agreed, to the disappointment of her mother and sister. In despair, she attempted suicide, driving her car off the road at high speed, but succeeded only in getting pursued by every law enforcement agent in the county. Though she was not hurt, she went to the state psychiatric hospital. When telling about her stay there, she recalled the life-saving music therapy that temporarily rescued her.

Soon after, she had a wrenching altercation with her mother. In anger, she loaded up her pharmacy of pills and drove for hours, before taking a hotel room. She sat in the room for four days with her pills spread out in front of her. Finally, she loaded everything up and went home. It came as no surprise that while she was gone, she had lost her job again. She graduated from nursing school in 1986, but had another major breakdown and landed back in the hospital.

Then in 1989, a lightning strike of good luck came from the most unlikely quadrant of the compass. Sarah was in the hospital again, depressed and suicidal, when she met Joe. Also a patient there, Joe was depressed over an unfaithful wife and a failed marriage. While Joe had his own struggles, he loved to laugh and he loved to listen to Sarah play the piano.

In Joe, her sweet love, Sarah had a man of smiles and encouragement. He was a man with x-ray vision that saw right through Sarah's depression and anger and pain, straight to her heart. He took vicarious pride when she played the piano, and he recorded her playing to share with their friends. He was able to pull her back from the perils of the night. But then he slipped away, dead from causes that would never be fully understood.

The weight of Sarah's grief exhausted her. Tired and sad, her old acquaintances, depression and despair, moved back in with every evidence they intended to take up permanent residence. She was not able to get her feet under her again. A new series of hospitalizations followed, and different prescriptions for new medicine were written, all to no avail. Fresh out of another stay at Red River hospital, Sarah had found herself sitting in front of me, starting all over again.

As Sarah completed her narrative and we sat before one another, she commented, "Do you know what you said in that first session that made me come back?"

"No," I said. "Actually, I don't remember a lot about the specifics of our first session."

"You listened to me talk about how hopeless my case was and that I didn't think anyone could help me. And at the end of the session, you kind of sat up a little taller in your chair and you looked at me. Then you said, 'Sarah, I know this sounds a little arrogant, but I just have a hunch that I can help you!"

"I said that?"

Sarah laughed, "Yes, you did."

I honestly didn't remember, but she recalled it with such confidence that I couldn't doubt her.

Early on, I usually try not to encourage rescue fantasies and begin to champion the patient's own wisdom about herself and her own resources for healing. But perhaps recognizing that Sarah was bereft of belief that she or anyone else could help her, I was only telling her I wasn't afraid to climb out on that limb, and I would believe for her until she could believe for herself.

The third epoch, a time of openness and progress, was born from the trust Sarah and I came to relish and in the relationship we created with the express mandate for her to defeat depression, to recreate relationships with others, and to find enduring peace and joy.

Up to that point, she was working on two goals, both regarding interpersonal contact. She was going to rid herself of the notion that she was worthy of rejection, that other people were eagerly waiting to dismiss or ignore her. The second was realizing that she had permission to end unfulfilling relationships and to seek out more fulfilling ones.

Many failures littered those months, as Sarah tried again and again to get a foothold in healthy relationships. But when she failed, instead of reeling back into despair, she would bring it back to the session and we would work on it. She began to accept that even if she was rejected, the world didn't end. She could pick herself up, learn the lesson, and try again. I was delighted when she actually began to laugh at herself in these moments, not in self-derision but in a light, lovely titter that lessened the significance of an issue and enlightened her to the fact that life would inevitably arrange a "do-over," and the next time she would do better.

The heart of the final epoch and the sign that our work was coming to completion involved, not surprisingly, the piano. Many other improvements had been made. Sarah and her sister had enjoyed a rapprochement, she was visiting her daughter, Abby, and the grandchildren, and she was learning to enjoy them without judgment or trying to "fix" what she didn't like. She was just letting them be who they were and loving them. She had gotten rid of a few toxic friends who seemed to have a special gift for bringing her down. She found new friends who she really seemed to enjoy, and who made her laugh, even if it was at how crazy they were. She began to travel all over the country to visit and renew old acquaintances and enjoy some new scenes for a while.

In all of this, she would occasionally have a bout of depression, but the episodes seemed to last a week or two, and then she'd be off again to live her life, avoiding hospitalizations or shock treatments. She took a modest antidepressant regimen prescribed by her psychiatrist, but the meds were stable and their effects consistent.

The piano was the only remaining intractable issue. She was still not getting the opportunity to play in church as much as she would have liked. She had used all of the techniques we had rehearsed to try to convince those in charge of the music program at the church that she really wanted to be used more at the piano, but in vain.

One day, as we were pondering this impasse, I said, "I wonder if this is a bigger deal than we have considered. We have treated this like an issue of assertiveness in dealing with those responsible for the music program, but maybe it's bigger than that."

"What do you mean?" she said.

"Well, I know your commitment to faith. Let me frame this in theological terms. I wonder if God has something else for you to do. Maybe what you are encountering at your church is simply a closed door. It has nothing to do with your skill as a pianist. It's not a referendum on whether or not you are a worthy person. Maybe you are destined for another path."

"Well, how do we find it?" she said, smiling at her own stubbornness.

Over the next few weeks, we revisited that idea. She didn't think she wanted to teach again. Playing for wedding and funerals was satisfactory, but not fulfilling.

It seemed that she was stumped. In a small town, there were only so many opportunities. In the past Sarah had lived reactively, and for her that meant a constant state of recoil from a world that seemed to reject her. But, she had changed. By actively seeking a solution, she had loosed a secret force, a secret power known to people who are proactive. A wise man, maybe J.W. von Goethe, more likely W.H. Murray, once said,

> *"Until one is committed, there is hesitancy, the chance to draw back. Concerning all acts of initiative (and creation), there is one elementary truth, the ignorance of which kills countless ideas and splendid plans: that the moment one definitely commits oneself, then Providence moves too. All sorts of things occur to help one that would never otherwise have occurred. A whole stream of events issues from the decision, raising in one's favor all manner of unforeseen incidents and meetings and material assistance, which no man could have dreamed would have come his way. Whatever you can do, or dream you can do, begin it. Boldness has genius, power, and magic in it. Begin it now."*

Sarah was beginning to lay down the burden of defending a fragile ego and open herself to others. She was radically accepting the pain of her past and embracing the life she had and that she was creating. Sarah was beginning to realize that she had the power to grace the world not only with the piano, but with her gifts of friendship and acts of compassion and generosity. It was no surprise to this old therapist when Sarah came in one day absolutely beaming. She sank into the couch and sat there, a vision of amazed happiness.

"Well, tell me! What happened?" I implored.

"David, I just can't believe it. One of the other Catholic Churches called me out of the blue. They heard I played the piano sometimes at my church."

She sat back, still smiling with something akin to astonishment. "They asked me to audition to play at the church and that's not even all. They want me to lead the choir and work with the lay minister to plan all the music!"

As I began smiling myself, listening to her glad announcement, I couldn't help recalling that angry, dark, resentful woman I had first met. Now, she was absolutely beaming, having just announced that her dream had been realized, and that life had actually smiled on *her*!

To this day, on any given Sunday, you can slip into the back of that little Catholic church, and you will notice beautiful music lifting heavenward. At the piano is a little woman named Sarah, whose hands are a blur as they race across the keyboard, whose eyes are closed, and whose mouth forms a smile. The smile proclaims that depression, rejection, pain, and loss will not prevail. It is a sign that nothing we cherish in life can ultimately be taken away from us.

I am not sure what made the difference with Sarah. I think it had little to do with me. Really, I just hung around and wouldn't leave. And I insisted on seeing her. She was never invisible to me.

> *Each of us, in our particular form, shares a divine spark, a little divinity. In some of us, that spark is not so easy to see, and some of us don't yet have the eyes to see it in each other.*

In the Christian tradition, human beings are not just creatures. Each person possesses the *imago dei*, the "image or likeness of God." Each of us, in our particular form, shares a divine spark, a little divinity. In some of us, that spark is not so easy to see, and some of us don't yet have the eyes to see it in each other. But as I looked at Sarah beaming that day, I was certain I was seeing it.

chapter nine

MOVEMENT THREE: MOZART'S STUDENT

Hope is the thing with feathers
That perches in the soul,
And sings the tune -
without the words
And never stops at all…

—EMILY DICKINSON

WHO WOULD YOU put forward as the best single representative in the history of mankind of who and what we are? Would you call on a moral or spiritual figure like Jesus, Mother Theresa or Gandhi? Or would you invite a thinker, perhaps Plato or Einstein? Perhaps you would choose an artist like Da Vinci or a writer like Shakespeare or Dickinson? Or might you just hold up a baby, any baby, and ask the judge to take a deep look into those eyes. All of us have surely been worth it when you look at our best, in spite of what we have done at our worst.

In the history of music, the short list would have to include Mozart. Mozart was so prodigious we almost need a new word for him alone. At the tender age of five, he was already composing music. He went on a concert tour with his father and sister when he was six. He was first published when he was nine. Ambitious and prolific, he composed hundreds of pieces in every musical form. He had a phenomenal ability to imbue in his operas complex psychological insight. At his death at the age of only thirty-five, he had composed twenty operas, fourteen masses, almost forty concertos, over fifty symphonies and twenty sonatas. Through his own amazing catalogue of composition and direct tutelage of other estimable students, he also influenced the music that would follow. I had the lucky chance to work in therapy with a sixth-generation musical descendant and devoted aficionado of the master himself.

Carol was sitting on her bathroom floor with her right hand clenching a bottle of beer and her left hand full of pills. Betrayal and rejection were crushing her, and panic was rising up, overwhelming her. Sobbing for hours in grief, she rehearsed the litany of people who had failed her. Her mother had, seemingly for her lifetime, constantly held her head beneath the surface of her impossible expectations. Her lover, so recently a source of hope and affirmation, had run back to her husband. Her so-called friends had hidden themselves away. One by one, they had disappeared, and here she was again, alone.

One more name was on the list of those who had betrayed her—God. The questions she was incessantly screaming at Him challenged Him to answer her same grim bottom line. *Why did you create me?! What were you thinking? What could possibly be served by making such a complete fuck-up?*

When her questions were met with silence, she held the bottle mockingly toward heaven, *That's what I thought!* She shoved a handful of pills into her mouth, washing them down with beer from the bottle. She gagged and choked, but did not relent until she had managed to swallow them all. After the first mouthful, a cold calm had descended. She repeated the ritual until the unholy host of despair was consumed.

She lay back and waited, not for absolution but annihilation—the sweet comfort of painlessness, of nothingness. Her head was spinning and her consciousness was beginning to slip away. Relief was on the horizon. She was on the edge of the unknown and she welcomed it gladly. *Finally, I'm free.*

Early on a Monday morning, I made a swing by an inpatient psychiatric hospital, where a psychiatrist and colleague had consulted me to provide a psychological evaluation of a patient. I found Carol eating breakfast in the cafeteria. An attractive young woman of Asian descent, she looked up with a pensive smile when she saw me approach.

After salutations, I introduced myself. "I'm Dr. Sabine. Your psychiatrist asked me to do a psychological evaluation with you, and I wondered if we could talk for a few minutes. I'd like to get to know you a little so I can put the data we collect from you in the proper context."

"Sounds okay," she replied.

Her smile and gaze were steady, not suggestive of sarcasm. Unlike the groan I often hear after I announce my intention to do psychological testing, she appeared eager to start the process. She had been hospitalized after a serious suicide attempt. I was surprised to find her so agreeable.

While she finished her breakfast, I started the interview. Carol was a social worker. From the onset, I could tell she was psychologically savvy. She spoke with insight and sophistication, and displayed an openness to reflect critically on her life. I liked her immediately.

I completed the evaluation over the next few days while she worked her way toward discharge from the hospital. In the process, I learned about Carol's journey to that confrontation with God and death on her bathroom floor. I also learned that the piano was a centerpiece of her life.

At six years of age, Carol started taking piano lessons. Her family bought a Yamaha upright piano with a rich dark brown finish and a beautiful tone. But Carol's relationship with the piano was not love at first sight. Her mother compelled her to practice an hour every day without fail. Friends who came to the door wanting her to play were sent away. A long time would pass before Carol came to appreciate that her mother was instilling important life lessons in self-discipline and dedication.

Among those who immigrate to America, Asian cultures tend to demonstrate hallmarks of persistence, tenacity, and a rigorous pursuit of excellence. What is worth doing is worth investing in it everything you have and all that you are. Carol's mother elevated these values to an art form, if not an obsession. Alongside Carol's natural musical proclivities, this contributed to a phenomenal learning curve in her acquisition of skill on the instrument. In spite of her growing ability, however, Carol remained a reluctant disciple. She said, "I was just a kid. The piano was not my friend."

Eventually, reluctance was overcome by the success she was enjoying at the instrument and the enjoyment she felt when she performed for others. By the age of sixteen, she was the winner of a major symphony orchestra piano concerto competition. She was the invited guest soloist in the symphony's performance of Mozart's Piano Concerto No. 12 in A major, K. 414, 1st movement.

"I remember warming up with scales on a grand piano in a large room directly below the stage where the symphony was performing its opening piece. When it came my turn to come onto the stage and sit at the piano, a shiny black concert grand with the richest tone I had ever played, I felt both nervous and confident. I'll never forget the power of the orchestra and how it made the floor vibrate beneath my shoes. My fingers flew across the keys and my heart soared with the music. Then came the applause . . . the flowers . . . the hugs backstage. That was one of the happiest nights of my life."

Upon graduating from high school, Carol went to the University of Texas at Austin where, ever the dutiful daughter, she double majored in music ("to please my mom") and pre-med ("to please my dad"). While at UT Austin, she performed two solo piano recitals and competed in piano concerto competitions across Texas.

Carol graduated with a Bachelor of Music in Piano Performance at the age of 23. She then went to the Pacific Northwest and began work on a Master's of Music degree in Piano Performance.

"I remember my life in the Northwest as a time of adventure, rain, excitement, rain, experimentation, and rain. I became an avid cyclist. I split my time between my studies, long practice sessions on the piano, teaching piano students, and long bike rides in the beautiful, scenic countryside."

I could not help noting the irony that this narrative of success and accomplishment was being delivered by a woman who just a few days earlier had almost succeeded in ending her own life.

Carol's rehearsal of her biography bore the unmistakable sweetness of nostalgia. I could not help noting the irony that this narrative of success and accomplishment was being delivered by a woman who just a few days earlier had almost succeeded in ending her own life.

"Carol, you must be very proud of your accomplishments. As you shared your story with me, I could see that several of those recollections still move you and make you smile in the telling of them. I am wondering how we got from those seemingly idyllic days to this one, here in the cafeteria of Red River Hospital. There must be more to the story."

"There is much more," Carol said obligingly. "My twenty-seventh year marked a change in my life. I can see now that I had been running for a long time, just not knowing it. I was not sure then what I was running from. I was dating a nice guy named Brian. I also had a friend named Maggie. I remember feeling what I could only call "strange stirrings" when I was with her. It was all very confusing. It was at that time that I had my first outburst of rage. I don't know where it came from, but one day in a fit of rage, I threw a stapler at my dean and stormed out, slamming the door both to his office and my academic career. I came back to Texas in shame and mortification, not understanding what was happening to me, but feeling that my life was suddenly and irreparably out of control."

Here and there in her story, and in her description of her family of origin, I began to detect a hint of something in Carol's style.

"Carol, would you say that you have a touch of perfectionism?" I asked.

Laughing, she agreed, but she said she had come by it honestly. "My mother is the quintessential perfectionist. And she demanded that of me. I am sure it is one reason for my success at the piano. She was relentless, driving me always to be better, to never accept failure. I owe a lot to her for pushing me to play and push myself farther."

As Carol talked about her perfectionism, I sensed that the same quality for which she had voiced gratitude was also her nemesis. In my pre-doctoral fellowship at Yale University, one of my mentors and professors was Dr. Sydney Blatt. Dr. Blatt was a prolific researcher and had a staggering number of studies published under his name, covering a variety of questions regarding both psychopathology and psychotherapy.

One day, Dr. Blatt summarized his research into perfectionism as a personality trait. He said that perfectionism is a difficult problem to address in psychotherapy, in part because it is not always seen as a problem. People who are perfectionistic accomplish a great deal and perfectionism is reinforced by a world that appreciates those accomplishments.

The problem is that perfectionists, by definition, are rigidly unable to accept failure. When failure is encountered, the perfectionist has an unparalleled "gift" for experiencing shame. A particular failure denotes not only a flawed action, but a flawed, defective person. The depths of that shame are difficult to overestimate. Carol had been born and bred into the fierce, uncompromising guild of perfectionism.

> *Perfectionists, by definition, are rigidly unable to accept failure. When failure is encountered, the perfectionist has an unparalleled "gift" for experiencing shame.*

One other point Dr. Blatt made was that even though difficult and sometimes time consuming, successful psychotherapy with the perfectionistic patient is not only possible, it is important. Perfectionists are hugely valuable to society and culture because they are inherently talented, and we are all the benefactors of their considerable gifts. However, they need to be able to modulate and modify their self-image.

Upon Carol's discharge, her psychiatrist asked if I would be willing to take her on as a psychotherapy patient. The next Monday, she came to my office for our first session together. I hoped that I was competent to help. I knew in this case, saying that the stakes might be life or death was not too melodramatic.

"Carol," I asked at the start of our first session, "how did you feel when you came around and realized your suicide attempt had failed?"

"Cheated, I suppose. I couldn't believe I had survived again. This was my fourth attempt. Maybe the first three were actually just gestures, cries for help or whatever. But this time I had resolved to get it done."

"What happened to prevent your resolution this time?" I asked.

"Some of the people I was friends with at work started to worry about me and came to check on me. My truck was in the driveway and the house was lit up. When I didn't answer, they almost broke down the door. I don't recall any of it, but they told me they found me passed out on the floor. I was taken to the hospital. From there, they transferred me to the psych ward."

"Are you still feeling suicidal, Carol?" I asked.

"No. I haven't since I left the hospital. But I know the drill. I don't have any means to do it. And I promise that if I start thinking about that again, that I will call you or contact you before I do anything to hurt myself."

"Okay, it's a deal then," I said. She obviously had often contracted with her own clients for their own safety at her job as a social worker. Now, she was once again on the other side of the contract.

"Carol, you sound very savvy about this process. I assume you have also been in therapy before?"

"Oh yes," she said. "My therapist, Jennifer, was awesome. We did great work together. I have not seen her since I moved here a year or so ago. She called me a couple of times, but I didn't call her back."

"What did you guys work on?" I asked.

"David . . . may I call you David?" she asked.

"Of course," I said.

"Well, David, I have a very conflicted relationship with my folks, especially my mother. Jennifer and I worked a lot on recovering from the trauma from my childhood. We also worked on my coming out. I am a lesbian, but I really came to deal with that late. Before that, I was engaged to a guy named Jordan. Right in the middle of our engagement, I came out to him. Oddly, we just sort of moved right into being best friends instead. In fact, he started to see Jennifer in therapy too. That got complicated for me."

No doubt very complicated. Her therapist was seeing her and her ex-fiancé during the same time period. Then, the therapist was writing her letters and calling on the phone after the therapy was terminated. Complicated indeed. At the time, Carol saw that relationship as extremely helpful, and she held the relationship with Jennifer in high regard. Later, I came to learn that Carol also struggled with feelings of anger, perceived rejection, and abandonment in the relationship.

"So how do you see our work together? What would you think is important for us to explore?" I said.

She mentioned two issues. "I think I need to explore both work and personal relationships, especially as they reveal a problem I have in dealing with fear of betrayal."

"Okay, and the other?" I queried.

"Religion," she said. "I have issues with God."

I had no problem considering whatever her issue with God might be. But in my experience, most people who raise issues in theological or religious arenas usually state the problem directly. *I'm worried about what happens when I die. If God loves me, why does God let bad things happen to me? I don't think God can love me because I have done things that are so bad.* But Carol's expression sounded personal, more like a relationship issue directly with God as opposed to some theological quandary. So rather than avoid Carol's issue with God when she brought it up in our first therapy session, I looked forward to it.

The manner in which Carol spoke of God led me to suspect that everything led back to the issue of abandonment. Whether in problems at work, in personal relationships, or in her understanding of God, it was Carol's experience that, just when she needed others to rescue her the most, she found herself deserted and alone, sometimes back on the bathroom floor with pills and booze. From the cold floor, she screamed at God. Even if it was wrath from God, she wanted a response, anything but that devastating silence. But even God did not seem to care. At least suicide offered the fantasy that she would be liberated from the pain of being so utterly unloved and alone.

As the session continued, Carol explained more about her work as a social worker at a state agency, serving clients with severe mental illness, work that she took very seriously. One of the contributing factors to her recent depression and suicide attempt was related to her complaining about a supervisor at work. Carol had filed a report alleging ethical misconduct. The actions of the supervisor had resulted in the abridging of a patient's rights, in Carol's estimation. The supervisor was notoriously difficult to deal with, but Carol thought she had to defend the patient who was being harmed. The matter had subsequently been resolved, and Carol was no longer in contact with the supervisor, but not in time to prevent a total breakdown. She had exploded in rage. Then, she was unable to bear her shame for the way she had reacted and her perception of her co-workers' critical judgment. She could not defend herself against the intensity of the conflict, and the collapse was complete.

As Carol recounted the circumstances of the conflict, I registered the ease with which I found myself pulled to defend Carol's actions. I wanted to plunge in and reassure Carol that she had acted nobly. After all, I knew what it was like to be misunderstood. I, too, on occasion have leaned into the strike zone and taken one for the team, only to hear the guys on the sideline, who were supposed to be grateful for my sacrifice, say "What team?"

I wanted to give in to the sweet indulgence of commiseration. But when I feel drawn to do some particular thing or take some action, especially early on in the therapeutic process before the patient is well known, I find it best to stand down and avoid the unspoken invitation.

I decided not to rescue her, but to wait. And I rested assured that, if I was right about Carol and right about me, this would not be the last time I would be invited to fill this role. I would have to be vigilant for her, for us.

Conversely, I needed to avoid responding in a way that sent the message that I was disinterested in or unconcerned about her struggle. That would only rehearse the old pain of abandonment. I needed to do or say something in between those two extremes of rescue or rejection.

"Carol, that sounds like a terribly difficult position to be in. I imagine you felt quite alone when no one came to your side. You wanted to defend the patient who seemed unable to defend himself, and at the same time, you wanted your co-workers to understand your motives."

"It was horrible," she said. "I have never felt so alone. No one seemed to care."

"Well, as we move ahead together," I said, "let's keep this dilemma in front of us. Maybe we can find a new path though those situations."

With that, we concluded our first session together. We hadn't had any particular epiphanies, but I thought we had communicated honestly. As far as I could tell, we had not rehearsed the patterns of the past, and we were laying the groundwork for the path to something new.

The next session, I picked up on the theme of Carol's rage.

"In the hospital, you told me about your life up until you were about twenty-six," I said. "That was when you had your first outburst of rage, right?"

"Yes, when I threw the stapler in the dean's office," she replied.

"Since you said your 'first' outburst, I presume there have been others."

"There have been others. And each seems to be followed by major withdrawal. I have thought about it, and I don't honestly know if the rages are a sign that I am just having a breakdown and the withdrawal is just another part of the process, or the withdrawal is because of shame over losing control. The episodes in my twenties and thirties seemed related to my struggle to come to grips with my sexual orientation."

After her first episode of consequential rage at the age twenty-eight, she dropped out of college and moved back to Texas. She regrouped and went back to her old university and enrolled in the Masters of Music program in Music Education. She became engaged to a man named Jake and taught a Bible study on the "Sins of Homosexuality."

However, her serenity was short-lived. "I blew up in rage again, and I dropped out of school for the second time. This time I broke off the engagement to Jake, and I quit playing the piano altogether. The piano had been a centerpiece of my life, but I didn't touch it again for five years."

The following year, she had the third outburst of rage. This time, she was being stalked by a lesbian. When she was overly aggressive in her confrontation with the stalker, Carol was arrested for assault with bodily injury, a Class A misdemeanor. The stalker was not charged, because the event took place before the enactment of Texas anti-stalking laws. Carol's arrest and subsequent criminal record took her to an unprecedented low.

"I was really just so ashamed and angry. I sat in my house, and just cycled down farther and farther into depression. I thought, 'I am a complete failure. I have brought disappointment and shame to my family. Of course, to Mom, that means shame to the entire Korean community, and the entire god-damn country of South Korea for that matter! What's wrong with me? Why am I so angry? Why do I stay all alone in my dark house with the phone unplugged, the door locked, and the shades drawn? Why didn't that crazy lesbian from work let me alone and quit stalking me? I'm not gay! I can't be. It's a sin against God. But what if I am? Talk about shaming the family. How could God love me if I am gay? I'm such a failure.

What's wrong with me? Why am I so angry? Why do I stay all alone in my dark house with the phone unplugged, the door locked, and the shades drawn?

I'm so tired. I can't do this anymore. You know what? Fuck it all. Fuck you, God! I HATE YOU, GOD!"

I watched Carol as she replayed her litany of rage. I could see how her shame had consumed her. Even as she recounted her thoughts, she tensed her jaw and spat out her words. The seething remained just beneath the surface.

"That's when I first attempted suicide. I took an overdose of pills and was hospitalized. The shame was just too much. After that, for the next few years, I tried again to be a model citizen, so back into the closet I went. I met and dated a guy named Jordan. We got engaged. The whole bit."

For a while, Carol's life was in a period of calm, at least on the surface. About four years after she was hospitalized, her parents surprised her with the gift of the family piano, the beautiful upright that she had played countless hours as a girl. The occasion was a bright spot in her memory.

"I couldn't believe it! My own piano! What a reunion, after five long years. I sat down nervously and touched the familiar keys. I started to play Mozart. For the first time in my life, I truly fell in love with the piano. I wasn't playing for a teacher, or a grade, or a degree, or as a job. I was playing for the sheer joy of playing, no pressure. I played for hours at a time, thoroughly engrossed in my music. I would lose track of time. Sometimes I played before even having my morning coffee, and I didn't stop until it got dark outside."

As ecstatic as those periods were for Carol, thrilled in the company of her beloved piano, they could not buffer her from the pain of the next decade. She broke off her engagement with Jordan and finally came out to everyone at the age of 35.

The significance and power of a homosexual person's decision to come out is without a parallel in heterosexual people's lives. Unless a person is especially resilient and robust in coping skills, disclosing to the world something so condemned by so many in the culture and at the same time so essential to a person's identity is a recipe for depression, or anxiety, or shame, or panic or all of the above. Carol knew she could no longer delay this leap into the unknown. She didn't know how anyone in her life would

> *The significance and power of a homosexual person's decision to come out is without a parallel in heterosexual people's lives.*

react. But the secrecy initially offering her protection was ultimately an acid that was eating away at her soul.

Carol might have fantasized that she would be offered a soft landing by those around her, but the reality was brutal. Her family disowned her outright. Neighbors and friends from church shunned her. After living in fear of abandonment, that fear was now realized. She was alone.

Unable to bear the abandonment, Carol stopped attending church and, for the first time in her life, she lost faith in God. Her isolation was complete. Two more suicide attempts followed, along with subsequent psychiatric hospitalizations.

In all of the pain and retreat of those years, there was one decision Carol made that perhaps was her salvation. Carol started going to psychotherapy with Jennifer, a therapist who was lesbian herself. She saw her for eight years. During that time, the unmistakable signs of growth and change became evident. She reunited with her family. She got back in school and graduated with a Master's of Social Work. She embraced her ethnic roots after a lifetime of internalized racism and shame.

In 2007, Carol was riding high with a new career. She moved to Texas to start her new job. In her own words, "I did it! After three attempts at graduate school, I finally got my Master's. I felt good . . . a personal victory. I developed insight into my issues and a higher level of self-awareness. I learned better coping skills. I felt confident I could help others now. I was excited, although a little apprehensive, moving to such a small town."

Carol's euphoria was an experience about both an arrival and a departure. She had arrived, it seemed, at a place of greater understanding about herself, a much more peaceful and congruent place. Eight years of therapy and a lot of hard work had paid off.

It was a departure, too. She was taking her new insights and skills and launching off into a new life. She was slipping the bonds of the past and was heading out to a little town in north Texas where she knew no one. Rather than panic, as she might have done in the past, she was excited at the prospects for adventure that lay ahead.

But the itinerary of the soul is mysterious. Its destinations are not written in black and white, but in the transient colors of emotion and perception. What seemed like our final destination just yesterday, appears today as just another stop along the way.

As a boy, I travelled along a path that was littered with a hundred destinations, each of which, upon arrival, I was certain was my final one. I was raised to view the world in only one way, through the lens of religious faith. Whenever I faced pain or failure or fear, I was simply told, "Take it to God."

Tender as I was, I did as I was taught. Whenever I took it to God, I would inevitably find ecstasy there. At the end of a church service or summer camp revival service, and at the minister's invitation, I would rush to the front of the church and kneel at the altar. In prayer and contrition, I was transported to a place of transcendence. And for a time, I soared over my problems that only minutes earlier had seemed insurmountable. Tears would flow, my heart would race, and I was in tune with the universe, connected to everything. From that vantage, it was all so beautiful.

In my innocence, I interpreted my ecstasy to mean that I had arrived in a new place and had resolved my problems forthright. After all, I had given them to God, and surely God could handle them.

However, in the parlance of Christian faith, you *have to come down from the mountain*. Inevitably, I would come back down. My brush with transcendence was only that, a fleeting relief. Within a few days, I was back in the soup of frustration, wandering down the road again, seeking a place I could finally call home.

> *The destination is always illusory. We are pioneers, not settlers; travelers, not tourists. There are always new levels for adventurous spirits to plumb, and we are at our best when we are moving.*

After years and countless iterations of this cycle, I realize that the destination is always illusory. We are pioneers, not settlers; travelers, not tourists. There are always new levels for adventurous spirits to plumb, and we are at our best when we are moving.

Thankfully, our wandering is not aimless. It is in response to a steady homing beam, calling us not to a destination, but to a journey. We are nomads, never at home, but always at home, because the whole world is home to us.

For Carol, her years of wandering had been in pain and insecurity. She had worked hard, dealt courageously with herself in therapy, and now had seemingly found the possibility for sustainable peace in that small town in Texas.

So when she had set up her life and embarked on her new and promising career, she was a bitterly disappointed to find that her tenacious old nemesis, rage, had somehow followed her there. Rage again opened the door for the others in the cast that always vexed her. Fear and shame rushed in and climbed, clutching and clawing, onto her back, just when she thought she had shrugged them off for good.

Finally, the old script was completed when Carol's dark relief, suicide, came knocking again too, with promises of rest from the never-ending cycle of futility that seemed to be her heartbreaking destiny.

Why was it that, in the face of pain and trouble, she was so inclined toward suicide? As I listened to Carol's story, two powerful and deeply inter-related forces converged.

One was her Korean heritage. Carol came to realize that she had been deeply unwilling to accept her racial and ethnic heritage. She had difficulty embracing many of the noble traditions characteristic of the culture. Ironically, she had been influenced by one of the more troubling aspects of that same culture.

In a statistical analysis by the World Health Organization in 2009, of the thirty-one industrialized countries assessed, South Korea was number one in per capita suicides by women. The many reasons for this are impossible to untangle, but undoubtedly, it is in part related to the fierce pride and pressure to succeed that seems endemic to the culture. Another reason was surely the historical role of women in the culture. In past generations, Korean society was patriarchal. Outside of their roles as wives and mothers, the status of women was in doubt.

The second force compelling Carol toward suicide was her mother's behavior. In 1975, Carol had been present when her mother had tried to throw herself off of a balcony after learning that Carol's father was having an affair.

As Carol watched her mother's suicide attempt in horror, she had little insight into why her mother had reacted in such a way. But her mother's own father had divorced Carol's grandmother. In Korean culture at that time, divorce often meant that the wife was expelled from the home with nothing, a complete outcast with no money or belongings. Her grandmother was even denied access to her own children. Carol's mother had lost her own mother in this way. Her mother later learned that Carol's grandmother had died alone of a brain aneurysm. Carol's grandfather, on the other hand, married his concubine, ("another old Korean tradition," according to Carol), which was particularly painful for Carol's mother because she had always considered herself to be a "daddy's girl."

Research into social learning theory has revealed that when a family member completes suicide, the chances are nine times higher that another family member will succumb to suicide as well. Carol's mother, in attempting suicide out of shame and fear, had unknowingly given her daughter a primer in self-destruction.

And so, here she was again, in spite of many positive gains and new insights, recovering from another suicide attempt. It was at this moment, when almost miraculously, bewildered and more than a little angry to be alive, Carol was starting over with a new therapist who knew nothing about her or her long journey to that point.

Not until I had heard her remarkable narrative from start to finish did I realize what an act of faith and courage it had taken for Carol to sit down with me and begin all over again.

Soon after we completed the several sessions in which we recounted her story, Carol came to the office with a stack of about 30 letters and sat them down beside her on the couch.

"I have been thinking about what we should talk about next," she said, "and I feel maybe we should work on my relationship with Jordan, my ex-fiancé."

Carol lowered her eyes and pulled the letters into her lap and let out a sigh. It was clear she was struggling with some ambivalence about what was to follow.

"All of these letters are from him. He wrote them to me from prison. I have been unable to open any of them. I just can't bring myself to do it."

I didn't know whether to ask first about why Jordan was in prison or why she couldn't open the letters. I waited for her lead.

"I would have to say, I have been as close to Jordan as anyone in my life. We have a lot in common, especially our love for the cats and dogs we have adopted. In fact, I have several of his cats and care for them every day while he is away. He has been there for me in some of the most difficult times of my life—and I haven't spoken to him in two years.

"David, the truth is that I don't know what to think of Jordan. I have been avoiding the issue for all this time. You see, I was the one who put him in prison, as surely as if I had slammed the door and turned the key."

I heard the pain in her voice and saw her eyes brim with tears. She took a tissue and paused to collect herself to continue.

"We had been together in one way or another for several years. Even when I came out to myself and to him that I was lesbian, he stood beside me. When my parents were driving me around the bend, he was stalwart and strong. I came to count on him being there in my life. I would have to say that I trusted him implicitly. The Jordan I knew was kind, intelligent, and fiercely loyal.

"Then a day came that brought it all down in one terrible moment. I was coming over to Jordan's house to check on the animals. We often helped each other out that way. I came tripping into his place like I had countless times before, like it was my own place.

"I remember I turned to close the door, and the cats started coming to me to say hello. I dropped down on the floor for a minute and loved on them. Then I looked up and saw that Jordan's computer was on."

Carol paused in her story for a moment, her eyes caught in a trance. For a moment she was so immersed in the memory that she didn't appear to know that I was there. But the look on her face was one of horror.

Without warning, her eyes darted, and she stared, unblinking, at me. I resisted again the temptation to rescue her, to change the subject to something less painful. I waited.

"David, the screen-saver was a series of pictures, pictures of children. It was child porn." With this, tears began to roll down her face.

"You hear about child porn, but I had never seen it before. And I never want to again. David, I only looked for a couple of seconds, but I can still see those precious girls made-up like grown women. And their eyes! Those eyes still haunt me. In those eyes I saw so plainly their fear and betrayal and humiliation.

"It wasn't long, maybe a few seconds, before it registered with me that this was not some random, unintentional pop-up. This was a disgusting screen-saver Jordan had made on purpose!"

Carol paused again. At that moment, the office, that had so often been like a sanctuary, now seemed funereal.

"Carol, I am so sorry," I managed to say. I wanted to offer so much more. I could see how devastated she was, but nothing else came.

She continued, "To have a relationship that had always been sustaining and meaningful shattered in a moment was so sad. Over the next few days, I agonized over what to do. Could I possibly ignore it? I was in my last semester of my Master's degree program, my third attempt. I was studying Social Work and I was committing my life to helping insure that the vulnerable ones among us were safe and taken care of. It felt like an incredible hypocrisy to do nothing.

"I also wondered about the possible consequences to me. If he was someday apprehended, and it was somehow discovered that I knew about it and did nothing, would I be considered an accomplice? Would I lose my license to practice social work?"

She looked again at the unopened letters from Jordan in her lap. Without raising her eyes, she said, "That's when I decided to turn him in. It was terrible to have to see your best friend charged with such an awful crime, but there was no alternative.

"The cops came and arrested Jordan. They seized his computer and found thousands of images and videos. He pled guilty and went to prison. That's when he started to write the letters. He wrote often at first, but when I never responded, he started writing less often. I still get one every month or two now."

"And you have never opened even one?" I asked.

"No, they are all here," she replied.

The two of us sat there looking at the envelopes. What did they contain? Was Jordan furious that Carol had turned her in? Was he asking for forgiveness? Was he in denial about the significance of what he had done, or was he taking responsibility?

"So you brought them with you today," I said. "What do you propose we do with them?"

"I don't know. I just know it's time to do something."

I had an idea. "Why don't you arrange them in order by postmark date?" I suggested. "When you are ready, we can open one here in session and read it. We can talk about the content of the letter and how you feel about it. If that is helpful, we can open the others."

"I do think it's time," she replied. "But I'm not sure I am ready today. Can we do it next time?"

"Of course," I said, "Let's start with one next time."

The next session was charged from the first moment. The letters were there, sitting beside her. In her trembling hands was the one postmarked first.

"Carol, I know you have had reason to leave these letters unopened. And you appear afraid. Why are you afraid to read the letters? Do you know?"

"I guess I am afraid of what he might say," she said. "But really, the idea that when I open the letters makes me think I am resuming the relationship with him in some way. I am listening to what he has to say. My M.O. has always been withdrawal and isolating. I have that down pat. I do it very well. When I was so hurt by Jordan and what I was forced to do, I instinctively pulled back to that place where I could cut myself off. It's the way I do things."

"Is that what you want to do now?" I asked.

"No. It's time," she said. She sighed deeply and neatly tore the end off of the first letter. She unfolded the three or four pages, and I could see they were hand written on both sides of the page.

Carol's smile was bittersweet when she saw his handwriting and she cocked her head and cut her eyes up toward me as if seeking encouragement or permission or something. I smiled back, hoping that she would know I was with her in this.

"You want me to read them to myself and then talk about them or do you want to read them first?"

"I want you to do this in whatever way seems right for you," I said.

She thought for a moment and then said, "I think I will read them out loud. That way we can both take it in together."

"Perfect," I said.

Tentatively at first, but soon with more confidence, Carol read his greetings to her, then an update on where he was, and a transfer to another facility that might be imminent. Then he asked about the pets. He asked about each one in turn, commenting on how he was predicting they were each handling his absence. Carol paused several times as she read that section, obviously touched by the shared familiarity in his words about the animals. He concluded by referring to her as his best friend, how much he hoped that she was well, and finally how much he would like to hear from her.

When she finished reading the letter, Carol lowered the pages and let them rest on her lap. She sat there silently.

"Well, how was that?" I asked.

Smiling, she said, "Not too bad."

For the remainder of the session we talked about all the feelings that had come along as she read. In one sense, each feeling was important. In another sense, none of them were important. What was important was that she was reading them. She was on the way. She was moving again.

Over the next few weeks, she read them all. At each letter, we experienced a recurring blend of emotions. For me, the blend was two parts curiosity, two parts excitement, one part dread. For Carol, dread dominated. So many fears surfaced as she contemplated what was in the letters. Would something be revealed that would make her recoil in anger or cause her to lapse into sadness or regret? She did discover in the course of several letters that a cherished friend had gotten sick and died. But more often than not, the letters hid no bombshells. Some were ramblings about the pets. Some talked about the absence of response from Carol. But he never pressured her to write back, or scolded her for not doing so. Sometimes he would talk about where he was or where he was being transferred next. For me, the most moving letters were the ones where he seemed honest about his transgressions and was trying to reconstitute something in himself that would allow him to go on. The letters in the late going were decidedly more spiritual and philosophical. The one subject that never came up was his pedophilia, what he thought about it, where it came from, and how he planned to address it when he returned to his life outside of confinement. Was he dealing with his problem or just avoiding the issue with Carol in an effort to protect her?

I confess that I found the letters beautiful at times and that I found myself admiring the way Jordan coped with imprisonment. He faced his incarceration without anger and without self-pity. He saw it as an inevitability and as an opportunity. I wondered if I could be as strong in the face of a challenge like that.

When the time came that Carol read the last letter, we had talked for hours about the relationship. As we summed up that part of our work, she said she felt relieved to have read them all and proud that she had done it. I told her I was proud of her, too.

Carol decided the last step for now in her relationship with Jordan was to write him back. "It's been several years . . . but it's time." She worked on the letter for several weeks. When she brought it in and read it to me, I thought it was wonderful. She updated him on what had happened in the intervening years, but more importantly, she processed her feelings about him, what he had done, and what she needed to do to take care of herself. She was generous and compassionate, but not excusing or minimizing the significance of his terrible choices.

Satisfied, she sealed the letter. "I'm glad that's done," she said.

Carol and I had spent several months reading and working with Jordan's letters. I wondered what was next for us.

Sometimes in psychotherapy, what is talked about is not as important as what is not being talked about. Over the course of a year, I had, on a few occasions, reminded Carol that she had mentioned *two* issues she wanted to address in our first session. The first was work and interpersonal relationships. The relationship with Jordan and his letters to her had taken center-stage, but from time to time we had spent sessions on other relationships, also.

> *Sometimes in psychotherapy, what is talked about is not as important as what is not being talked about.*

What we had not talked about was the issue of God. Wanting to respect whatever was Carol's resistance, I had never pressured her. I would mention it in passing every few months. She would typically acknowledge that she, indeed, wanted to discuss the issue of God, and then she would move right back to Jordan or some other issue. It was clearly difficult for her to break ground on the situation with God, but I wasn't sure why.

Finally, after a year, I decided to take the direct approach.

"Carol, I notice that we have been working together a while now, and we still have never broached your issue with God, or religion, or whatever. I don't want to pressure you to talk about it. This is your time. You can use it anyway you wish. If you like, we can take that issue off of our agenda. Perhaps you don't think it is important enough to work on. If that is so, it is fine with me. But I know you are familiar with the idea of 'resistance' in therapy, I have wondered if we might be dealing with a bit of that in this instance."

Carol smiled, "No, you are right, I think. It is important, but I have been fearful about opening that can of worms."

Trying to reassure her, I said, "Well, you needn't feel pressure from me about God. But maybe instead of talking about the issue now, we could talk about where you think the resistance comes from. What is it that you fear?" I asked.

"It's you," she said plainly.

Me? I thought. This surprised me. As far as I knew, I was totally open to work with her on the "God" issue. How could I be the problem?

I said my thought out loud, "Me?"

"The truth is, David, that you have become quite important to me. Since we started working together, I have had struggles in my life, but not like before," she explained. "I have not returned to that place where I wanted to die. In fact, I am feeling more and more in control of my emotions, and that is encouraging to me."

"I'm very happy you are feeling better and that you feel positively about our work together. Frankly, I feel the same way. But I'm still confused. How am I the problem?"

"Well, I'm not saying that there is something wrong with you or that you are doing something wrong. It's just that opening the religion issue involves a question I have for you, and I'm afraid of the answer. Therefore, I've simply been afraid to ask."

As Carol spoke, her question for me suddenly came to me. I had worked with many gay people through the years and a particular conundrum about God and religion reliably surfaced, especially from those with a more conservative religious upbringing. I knew that the powerful question could set the stage for either shame and self-loathing, or liberation and self-acceptance.

I grabbed a small whiteboard and picked up the pen. I wrote a sentence on it, hidden from her view.

Carol looked down at the board curiously, then back at me. "What did you write?" she inquired.

"I hope I am not trying to be clever here, but if I know your question, which I think I do, I have written my answer on the board. I may be wrong, which would be a bit embarrassing. But if I am right, I wanted to write my answer down even before you ask it, because then you will know my answer was not influenced by anything. I will be giving you my honest opinion."

Carol was intensely focused on what I was saying. She appeared fearful, which reinforced my notion that I had the right question.

Carol waited in silence for a moment. Then, she tentatively began, "Well, my dad is on the board of regents for a Christian college, and my family has been active in church for all of my life. In the last few years, since I have come out as a lesbian, I have not been to church much. And my parents fear that I am lost. In fact, I don't even know what to make of my spiritual life these days. I think it's pretty much empty. I think God and I are not on speaking terms.

"Over the past year, you have alluded to the fact that you, too, were raised in church and that you have been to seminary. That has made me curious about this question. . . "

Carol hesitated, her brow furrowed in worry and apprehension.

I again wanted to rescue her. I wanted to do the talking and let her off the hook, but I resisted. She needed to ask.

She gathered herself, and let out a sigh. "Do you believe homosexuality is a sin?"

We sat for a moment with the issue that had been between us, now in the open and demanding an answer. I was important to Carol, and my response mattered. I had been encouraging her to accept and love herself. But what if I believed that homosexuality was essentially not acceptable to God?

We were poised for a moment of breakthrough, although, as usual, I was not immediately aware of it. I thought I was just making a point of clarification, perhaps a little too dramatically. I didn't see the significance of this unusual moment.

Without saying a word, I reached for the white board and turned it around to face Carol. She burst into tears of relief as she read, "Homosexuality is not a sin."

My own eyes welled up as I shared in her relief. I also shared candidly with her how I came by my belief.

The first time I wept in a session where I was the psychotherapist, it troubled me a little. Maybe it didn't seem professional. Maybe it signaled I was too enmeshed with the client's feelings. Maybe my tears would frighten the client, thinking I was having a breakdown.

These days, though, a week rarely goes by when I don't weep in a session along the way. Sometimes tears come because of a grief that descends on the room. Sometimes they come as I listen to a client's story and hear him or her state feelings out loud for the first time, having lived for years under the censure of shame and humiliation. Sometimes it is a moment of *Kairos* where the breathtaking beauty of life peeks through and I just can't help myself.

> *My tears are one way the clients come to understand that I am with them. I am not shrinking from their pain. Although I can't fix it, it still matters to me.*

My tears are one way the clients come to understand that I am with them. I am not shrinking from their pain. Although I can't fix it, it still matters to me.

With Carol, my tears caught me by surprise. I had not been conscious of this matter between us, but now I could see that it had been there the whole the time.

Carol and I indisputably had a close relationship, characterized by openness and honesty. But unbeknownst to me, a potentially divisive issue had been standing between us. Like many impediments to the therapeutic alliance though, as soon as it was revealed, in the next moment it was wiped away. She had accepted the invitation and found the courage to draw near.

To "draw near" is a phrase that is deep and ancient. Throughout ancient scripture, the seeker is asked to "draw near," or "be still." or "sit down here." "I am like fire. As fire gives heat to those who draw near it, . . . even so do I." (Srimad-Bhagavad-Gita, Ninth Chapter) "Draw near, and fear not." (Koran, Sura 28: [31]) "Draw near to God, and God will draw near to you." (James 4:8, Holy Bible).

The power of love expressed in the enfolding of a mother's arms is unfathomable. It goes to the center of life, of love, and of all existence.

Ostensibly, the command to draw near is for the purpose of information or wisdom that is about to be whispered. But there is real magic in the simple command of draw near. The seeker is really and literally being invited to come closer to that which is the heart of all longing, the wisdom of all wisdom, where words are sometimes secondary, if they are needed at all.

Everything that needs to be said is there in that embrace as child and mother again occupy the same space, and the protection and warmth of the womb is for a moment reconstituted.

When the child who has fallen, who is cut and bleeding, sees her mother's open arms and hears the words, "come here," something happens that is far more comforting than the mother's reassuring words that everything will be okay. When the child *draws near,* she gets close enough for mom's arms to reach around her and enfold her. The power of love expressed in the enfolding of a mother's arms is unfathomable. It goes to the center of life, of love, and of all existence. In that caress, the mother might speak words of comfort, or she might say nothing at all. Everything that needs to be said is there in that embrace as child and mother again occupy the same space, and the protection and warmth of the womb is for a moment reconstituted.

Psychotherapy is a similar process. From the very first moment, the therapist and client set out to draw near to one another.

Psychotherapy is a similar process. From the very first moment, the therapist and client set out to draw near to one another. There are a host of obstacles that try to intervene. *I don't know you. You are different than me. You will judge me. You might hurt me. I pay you to do this, so this can't be real.* One by one, these hurdles are overcome, if both parties are sufficiently courageous. The therapist and the client draw near to one another, and in doing so, they tap into the essence of life, moving into that generative flow from which issues lasting peace.

What settled in place that day with Carol and me was the experience of drawing near to one another. The wall came down, and as the initial relief subsided, peace settled on us, sending out deep roots. From an exile born of countless disappointments, hope, Emily Dickinson's "feathered thing," flew in the window and lit on us, as if it had just come from a long trip and was home again.

Carol acknowledged the experience of *drawing near* this way: "David, when I first came to see you, I have to admit, I was dubious. I was used to Jennifer, who was a woman and also lesbian. On the face of it, you and I are so different. You are a man. I am a woman. You are heterosexual. I am homosexual. You are a white guy. I am of Asian descent. We come from two very different cultures. But now, I am blown away by how connected we are, with how much I see us now as somehow the same."

I, too, sensed that connection. Carol was beginning to feel at home in the room, and she seemed to really like who she was there. All that remained was for Carol to realize that it wasn't the room at all. And it was not me. *It was her.* She was not alone and never had been. Therefore, she could never be ultimately abandoned. When life brought pain, when she was betrayed by others; when she was tired and didn't think she had the strength to go on, she only had to *draw near.* Like Dorothy in the *Wizard of Oz*, she could close her eyes, click her heels, and be home again.

Home was no longer the house of her youth, with her mother, ever-vigilant and demanding, requiring perfection. Home was not a place of reminders of her failure to complete her parents' dream.

Home was now an internal destination, where Carol could go whenever she was scraped up and bruised by life, and where she could hear the magical incantation, "Draw near!" In astonishment, she recognized that sometimes, when she least expected it, life appeared impossibly beautiful and sweet. She realized then that she was actually experiencing one of those rare and precious moments when Life had taken the initiative and actually drawn near to *her*. She had come to understand that the invitation to draw near was an open one. She could be there at any time and be welcome. Home was instinctive, indelible—inscrutable, yes, but as real as anything else in her life.

Carol sits at the piano, no one else around. She pauses, hands ready over the keys. Her eyes close and her fingers play the first few notes of the concerto, written centuries ago by Wolfgang Amadeus Mozart when he was a young lad. The music emanates flawlessly through the room and out into the world.

Carol is connected *to* Mozart. Her teacher is a sixth-generation direct descendent, from student to teacher, of Mozart himself. On another level, she and Mozart both have histories of painful, emotional travails.

Carol is also connected *with* Mozart. As his written music flows away from Carol's hands, it also flows back to her and through her. She no longer thinks about individual notes, and she doesn't think about striking certain keys. She enters the piece, enfolding it and unfolding it in rich variations of mood and emotion.

Like Mozart, Carol is one of the lucky few who can actually enter into a musical composition and draw near enough to look through to the other side, past doubt and deficiency, past disappointment and failure. She is truly Mozart's student.

In her own words, "Life is a roller coaster. I've been stable the past two years. I like where I am now, and where I seem to be going. I enjoy helping others learn about depression. I find it gratifying to give back. I'm proud to be a social worker. I'm proud to be Asian. I'm proud to be lesbian. I'm proud to be a pianist. I still play my Yamaha, this piano that's been with me since I was six years old. My dear old friend. I play for the elderly residents at an assisted living center. I've reconnected with my family. I'm renewing my faith in God. I have hope.

EPILOGUE

Before the quiet comes…

AS YOU HAVE EXPERIENCED these stories from the perspective of my chair, in that inner sanctum of human experience, I hope you have encountered your own moments of *Kairos*. I hope you were reminded of what a wondrous thing it is to be human, even with all of our pain and problems.

In these past fifteen years, I have labored to help each patient find his or her way to that encounter, not with me, but with Life. It has been a labor of love.

Now, because of congenital and progressive hearing loss, I stand to lose that which I consider to be the essence of myself—my ability to listen. Beethoven, the great composer who lived shortly after Mozart, famously struggled, like I do, with tinnitus and hearing loss. He continued to compose even after he was completely deaf and his *Ninth Symphony,* one of the most beloved and well-known musical compositions in all of history, was created after he had entirely lost the ability to hear. It is poignant that millions upon millions have thrilled to his setting of "Ode to Joy" in that work, but the composer himself never heard it.

I am no Beethoven, but if he can compose music without the benefit of hearing, surely I can write. I am not morbid or fearful as I look ahead to that day when silence arrives for good. If my patients have taught me anything, it is this: Life always finds a way.

For now, I have much to do, and so do you my friend, before the quiet comes. . .

A Conversation with David Sabine, Ph.D.

1. Before you became a psychologist, you were a minister. What made you leave the ministry? Why did you choose psychology? And how did being a minister inform your practice of psychology?

Right, why go from the pulpit to the chair? My first assignment as a minister was to create an urban ministry in Fort Worth, Texas with a co-pastor, Bryan Stone. As I carried out those responsibilities, I noticed that Bryan naturally focused on the administrative and visionary aspects of the work, while I found myself sitting with my parishioners, listening to them and counseling them. I became fascinated and sometimes troubled by the way people behave and the choices we make. Eventually, I applied and entered graduate school in psychology, and became a psychologist. In my view, I have never left the ministry. Even though I work now as a psychologist, I am still giving expression to my gifts and my call to serve others. It's just the language that has changed. I don't trade directly in the currency of theological language, but I am still helping others find their way to meaning, to joy, to discover that they have a unique place in life, and to experience that belonging for themselves.

2.   Confidentiality between doctor and patient certainly extends to the relationship between psychologist and patient. How did you resolve that issue in writing your book?

The issue of confidentiality was a major concern in writing this book. I discussed the idea with each of the living major characters. I then had a series of meetings to ensure their comfort with my treatment of their story and the strategies I employed to conceal their identities. While it is certainly a high moral value to protect the confidentiality of the patient, it is also important for the larger culture to understand what goes on in the process, both to be assured that the process is humane and healing, and also to know what may be possible for those who struggle. A long tradition exists in both medicine and psychology/ psychiatry of recounting cases for the purpose of training and exploration as long as the identity of the patient is shielded from the reader. The patients who were the subjects of these stories were included in the process, and many asked for changes to be made to the original manuscript. We explored how they might feel knowing their stories were out there in such an enduring way. I wanted to ensure that the benefits of sharing their stories far outweighed any potential harm to them. I was impressed, but not surprised, that they each expressed a hope that their experiences would be healing for someone else who might be struggling with similar issues. It speaks to the kind of people they are.

3.   When listening to your patients, how difficult is it to remain impartial? What happens when you find it impossible to do so?

The most dangerous therapist is one who thinks he or she is impartial. Bias creeps in. Our prejudices are often beneath the surface. I know I am affected and limited by my own experiences, and the best I can to is remain vigilant for my biases, to watch for them, and insofar as possible to purge myself of them. I often will tell on myself with my patients when I catch myself projecting my own "stuff" onto them. Integrity in psychotherapy is a "verb." By that I mean it is active, a process, not something static I bring to the session. It is something that I hammer out moment by moment as I confront my own weakness, pettiness, and judgment on behalf of my patient.

4.   Have you ever had a patient you absolutely could not help? If you did, how would you handle the situation?

Over the past 15 years, there have been many patients I failed to help, if by help we mean that the presenting problem was resolved. In another way, I hope that every patient is helped by the experience of being esteemed, valued, and yes, I would even say, loved. Sometimes there can be healing even if there is no cure. That said, if I find myself stuck in a case, and I have reasonably tried everything I know to get the process moving, I seek out my professional colleagues to see if they can help me find where I am failing to really hear and be present with the patient in a more effective way. Most of the time, I call either James Walker, Ph.D. or Dan Wolverton, Ph.D., two brilliant psychologists who have been especially effective in helping me get "unstuck." If consultation fails, I will talk with the patient about transferring to another therapist, and if they are agreeable, I facilitate the transfer.

5.   How do you, or do you manage to, keep your personal beliefs separate from your professional interactions? Can you remain impartial?

Since the supreme value of my work with patients is a radical respect for them and their own lives and experiences, my own beliefs are just another source of ideas, options, and directions that stand alongside many others to their potential benefit. I do not presume to know what direction their lives should take. I only commit to help them explore their options, to cultivate their own resources, and then gather the courage to accept the adventure of their own unique lives. My own religious beliefs assist rather than interfere with the process. I view God as the great cosmic mystery that is not "out there" but in here, in every aspect of our lives, and I believe that the Mystery calls every person with a steady homing beam that is unique to them. I don't know their particular path, but I can sometimes see when a person is stepping in the direction of their own personal calling, and when that does happen, it is truly thrilling. So yes, I have my own distinctive beliefs, and those beliefs inform everything I do, but I hope those beliefs are expansive, not limiting.

6.   How does the view from your chair differ from the view of a friend or family member trying to help someone with a problem?

A friend or family member trying to help someone is quite different because the loved one or friend is always involved, and often enmeshed in the relationship. While the patient typically brings in the same issues to me that they display out there in their lives, the psychotherapist is expressly seeking to help the patient find new approaches to the old problems. Also, the confidential nature of our interactions offers the patient the opportunity, if he or she is sufficiently courageous, to be open, honest, and deal in a more direct way with their problems in life. Friends and family members may love the patient in powerful ways, but it is always in that context, as a mother, or sister, or friend, etc. In this relationship, the patient doesn't have to worry about taking care of me. The focus can be, without distraction, on the problems the patient brings into the therapy. The patient has a partner whose express reason for being in the conversation is to help him or her face their fears, their dysfunction, their dilemmas, the things that are not working well in their lives, and make the requisite changes that will result in a greater measure of joy in life.

7.   It is said that suicide is the ultimate selfish act. Do you believe this to be so? Why or why not?

No, I don't believe such a sweeping statement about such a complex behavior as suicide is either fair or accurate. Although some suicides are motivated by revenge and anger, as a way to "have the last word" and to torment the person or people left behind, it is often the product of deep depression. In such a state, a person may come to believe that everyone, sometimes including one's own children, would be better off not having them around. Others are so demoralized that they have lost all hope of meaningful life. Still others may be responding to psychotic thoughts or hallucinations compelling them to self-destruction. Finally, some simply want to make the call regarding whether or not they want to live and see it as a personal right, an extension of the right to self-determination.

8.   Do you ever lose patience with your patients? Do you ever want to point out that life is just not that bad for them?

I rarely lose patience with a patient in any observable way. More problematic is when I lose patience in a subtle way that gives no immediate feedback to the patient. When this happens it begins to poison the work and the relationship. So it is important for me to remain vigilant to feelings of strained patience, and if I am courageous enough to say it out loud, the patient and I can explore why I am feeling that way. It is not necessarily the patient's fault at all. Most often, it is my own failure, and telling on myself with the client allows me to reset my stores of patience and try again.

9.   Whether it is with eating disorders, cutting, or a host of other activities, self-abuse is rampant. Why do people resort to self-abuse and what is the key to helping them to stop?

While it is true that these behaviors all result in self-harm, they are not always self-abuse. Anorexia nervosa, for example, was long thought to be associated with controlling parents and a need to reassert control on one's life. Actually, the disorder is part of a broad spectrum of disorders that range from autism to compulsive gambling, and it has a lot more to do with a person's "hard-wiring" and neurotransmitter substances than his or her parents or particular life experiences. That is not to say, though, that some people don't use their eating habits to try to exact penance from themselves or to manipulate others.

Alcoholism appears to be, in part, due to a person's response to rising cortisol levels in the brain and the ability of alcohol to stimulate pleasure centers in a very primitive area of the brain, temporarily relieving the negative effects of the cortisol. The result may be harmful to the patient, but the intent is not primarily self-harm. On the other hand some people may decide to get drunk out of a need to punish themselves for some perceived failure.

Another example of apparent self-abuse is cutting, one of the themes of the second chapter. Cutting is always multi-caused, but it also has a biological component. When the person cuts, endorphins, the natural opiates produced by the brain, are released and this pleasurable consequence is often a prime motivator.

These behaviors are complex and seem to occur at the place where our biology and psychology merge. So helping patients to stop often involves a combination of psychotherapy and medical intervention. Medicine can help the patient by suppressing the symptoms that have them mired and by providing fledgling motivation to implement the strategies provided in psychotherapy that may lead to an enduring cure.

10. Why do you believe people turn to psychotherapists?

Master therapist Jerome Franke, Ph.D. M.D., after years of work in the therapist's chair, contended that patients come to psychotherapists in a state of demoralization. They have become stuck in their lives and problems and have lost hope and confidence in their own abilities to resolve their problems, to get moving in their lives. The therapist provides a "healing myth," a roadmap or frame that the patient and therapist can use to restore hope and belief in the patient's ability to transcend their problems. He used the term "myth" to indicate that there is no absolute truth or perfect path to follow in any objective sense. Rather, therapists may come from varying theoretical orientations and still be helpful to the patient. The path need only be clear, make sense to the patient, and be agreed upon as a path out of the patient's unique wilderness. I agree with Franke. This is why many therapists, myself included, contend that, in a broader sense, it is the relationship that heals. The particulars don't matter as much as the convergence of two committed people who pursue with courage and honesty an agreed upon path to healing.

11. As you see it, what is the job of a psychotherapist?

You asked me to express the job of a psychotherapist "as I see it." What follows is not what I would have written in response to a test question in graduate school, but is an expression of my own experience in the therapist's chair after thousands of encounters with patients. This is how I see it:

The psychotherapist is an apologist of meaning in human life. Historically, apologetics is the defense of a religious doctrine or belief. It refers to philosophical reconciliation. Religious apologetics is the effort to show that faith is not irrational, that believing in it is not against human reason. Psychotherapy is about existential reconciliation. The patient presents the therapist with problems and crises that challenge the assertion that life is meaningful. The therapist, in response, represents by his or her very presence and also by his or her manner of dignifying and affirming the value of the patient, that, far from meaningless, the patient's life and experience is laden with meaning. Beyond the apparent meaninglessness of a given problem or loss, life still has meaning, even though it may be up to us to create it. The painful experience of the patient is reconciled with the essential goodness and beauty that underlies everything. In the end, it is not irrational to believe in and create meaning. It is human to do so.

When you get down to it, we all want to count, we all want to matter, we all want to have a place in the scheme of things. To feel that we don't abrogates the meaning in our lives. Reminding the patient that he or she does have a place, that that place is worthwhile, is a reaffirmation. "It's all good" is a phrase repeated almost daily, but it's true when you look deeply enough.

12. What do you hope readers take away from reading your book?

Like I indicated in my answer to the last question, I am an apologist, a defender of the meaning of and in human life. My mission, my career, is sharing the good news that beyond the apparent, and sometimes brutal and devastating evil and pain of life, there is an essential goodness that not only defeats that evil and pain, but utterly overwhelms it. When that beauty comes into full view, pain and loss and grief and death are all transcended. From that vista, joy and peace pervade the landscape.

I do not presume, in this book, to offer a full defense or an exhaustive explanation of the meaning of human life. In the telling of these stories, I only intended to sample from the wellspring that rises from the center of the earth, to give the reader a taste of the depth and beauty of life as it is particularly revealed through the remarkable process of psychotherapy. I don't have this all figured out. I have just been transfigured by the experience, and I am compelled to bear witness to the sublime mystery of Life in the particular facets reflected through these ten souls.

"When I despair, I remember that all through history the ways of truth and love have always won. There have been tyrants, and murderers, and for a time they can seem invincible, but in the end they always fall. Think of it—always."
MAHATMA GANDHI (1869 - 1948)

Discussion Guide

Prologue

NOTE TO FACILITATOR: *The author's office is described in some detail in the prologue, and he talks about how he wants his patients to feel welcomed in all five senses. Consider ways you can offer your fellow discussants the experience of being welcomed in all five senses. It might be a point of conversation to set the stage for the group experience. Helping people attune to their sensory experience often opens the door to other, deeper destinations.*

What do you think of when you hear the word psychotherapy? How is therapy portrayed in movies and on TV? What do you believe is the difference between that portrayal and reality?

The author talks about the idea that in therapy it is the relationship that is the primary source of healing. Can you think about a time when a relationship with someone else was particularly healing? It might not be what the other person said, and not some advice they offered, but the relationship itself, how the two of you together were better than either of you all by yourselves.

Chronos and Kairos were kinds of time described in the prologue. Can you identify and share examples of each from your own experience?

Do you think there is something unique about psychotherapy, or is it just another way some people choose to address their problems? Share your thoughts about why or why not? If it is unique, what are its distinctive qualities? How is speaking with a therapist different from sharing with a close friend?

How did you feel when you began to consider that you were being invited into the therapies and lives of real people? What ethical considerations are involved in telling stories based upon the confidential discussions of a person and their therapist? What potential pitfalls should be considered?

Chapter One - The Box

Almost everyone has heard of people who cut on themselves. The author offers some common reasons given by those who do. What reasons do you think might commonly motivate those who cut their own skin?

Do you know anyone who has cut? Does Rose share personality traits with that person, or are they quite different?

Rose struggled, as most patients in this book did, with shame. How do you define shame? Do you think shame is a common enemy for many people? Does *everyone* struggle with it in some way? How about you? How does it show up and what do you do to cope with it? Are there negative or ineffective strategies you have tried to cope with shame?

Sometimes we hear of people who do quite radical things to cope with their emotional pain. Often those people seem very different from us. As you read about Rose, how did you feel when you learned how far she had taken her compulsion to cut? How did you feel at the chapter's end?

Chapter Two - Lillie Belle

It was important for Lillie to be remembered. Is that important to you? Imagine you are at your own funeral, able to observe the service. As the minister gets up and delivers your eulogy, what do you want said? Finish this sentence: "Remember me as . . ."

What does your response tell you about your priorities in life?

We live day to day with a pretty consistent personality. Our identity is based largely upon those traits. What might the consequence be of an event like a stroke or a traumatic brain injury to a person's identity, their sense of self? If you believe in a soul, is the soul subject to being changed as a result of a physical injury?

The loss of a child is considered by most to be about the worst grief imaginable. Lillie lost three of her four children to death. How does someone bear such a loss?

"A person's greatest strength is often also his or her greatest weakness." Do you believe that statement is true? Why or why not? When the author went to see Lillie for the first time at the hospital, she was routinely throwing therapists out of her room. To be that stubborn and hard to please is a liability to her best interest, right? How did those same qualities serve her through the rest of the story?

Chapter Three - Once to Die

Daniel was stuck in his grief. Have you ever tried to help someone who was grieving? What seemed to help? What was ineffective?

What, if anything, does grief do for us?

What do you think of the "near death experiences" you have heard about? What do you think is going on in those reports? Are they valid reports or something else?

What experiences have you been through that at first seemed unequivocally bad, but later turned out to be important for you in some way?

When the author encountered two people with pacemakers just after his own experience, was that just a coincidence or something else? How do you view such rare or seemingly unlikely occurrences when they appear in life?

Chapter Four - On the Razor's Edge

The author indicates that this story has been waiting for over two decades to be told. Have you had experiences that took time to understand? How did they indicate that it was time to approach them again?

Daryl and the author appeared to have a special connection. What was it? Was it good or bad?

At what points might the author have taken a different path or made a choice that might have changed the outcome? What lessons should one take from his failure?

Is it ultimately possible to prevent someone from committing suicide?

How did you view Daryl after reading the first four or five pages? Did your view change by the end of the chapter? If so, in what way?

How can a family cope with such a terrible and complicated loss? What emotions are associated with losing a friend or family member to suicide?

Why do people commit suicide? And is it, as some contend, the ultimate act of selfishness?

Connor was the son of Daryl and Robin. After the deaths of his parents, he was whisked away by his mother's family, probably to be adopted by Robin's sister. By all indications, they raised him without any knowledge of who his real parents are. Should they have kept the truth from him? Do you think he should read this chapter at some point in his life? Do we all have the right to know our background, good or bad? Why or why not? How might knowing impact him?

Chapter 5 - The Woman in the Yellow Mask

The author is direct in describing his first judgment of Agnes as "ugly." Did that make you uncomfortable? Should he admit that opinion, even if is true? Was it at best an error in judgment or at worst disrespectful to describe her in such negative terms?

Do you agree that "ugliness" is the great unspoken prejudice? What evidence would you bring to support your opinion?

If you were the therapist for Agnes, how would you have handled her antics? Ignore them? Confront them?

The author refers to his practice of trying to find that thing in a person that he values, that he loves. Have you known people that were a challenge in terms of your finding that thing to value and respect? How did you deal with that? In the end, was it that they had nothing to offer or that you simply were unable to discover it, perhaps because of your own limitations?

Again, if you were Agnes' therapist, would you have read the chapter to her in its entirety, or would you have left out the less flattering passages? Why do you think he chose to read it all?

Chapter 6 - Notes from the Inferno

The chapter about Betty begins with a letter in which she announces a plan to take her own life. If a friend wrote such a letter, what would you be inclined to do?

What experience have you had with pain? Have you ever dealt with chronic pain? If you have, how did you cope? If not, think of someone you know who lives with pain all the time. How do you think they cope with it?

Unlike a cast on a broken leg or some other visible evidence of a physical problem, pain most often cannot be seen. Can we ever fully empathize with someone else's experience of chronic pain? If not, how does that affect them?

Do you think there is such a thing as "rational suicide?" Are there times when it is morally acceptable for a person to decide they want to die and to act on that decision?

Are all people who want to commit suicide mentally ill?

Do you think it would be okay for the author to correspond regularly with Betty even after she moved to Scotland? Why or why not?

What do you think the author should have done when he received that first letter, informing him of Betty's plan to end her life? What would you have done?

Chapter 7 - Movement One: In the Shadow of Van Cliburn

Have you ever given up something you loved just because it became too painful for you for some reason? Did you ever go back to it?

Shame emerges again in this chapter as a powerful enemy. What would you have said to Josh to help him combat his shame?

How did you feel about the author's directly stating his opinion about homosexuality and the longstanding cultural bias about people who are gay? Was that necessary to the story or was the author just using the opportunity to have a "soap box" moment?

What are your opinions about the ethical issues that surround the topic of homosexuality? How did you come by those opinions?

Why does homosexuality engender such strong opinions? Why is it the topic of so much debate?

Was it ethical and/or professionally responsible for the author to invite Josh to the author's home to play the piano? Why do you believe he did so? What impact do you believe this had on Josh?

Chapter 8 - Movement Two: From Invisible Woman to Imago Dei

Sarah is introduced as filled with anger and self-pity. As you read her story, what do you think were the sources of these feelings?

As you read the account of Sarah's struggle with her ex-husband, what did you feel and think about her daughter being taken from her over and over again? Was it right? How would you handle that situation?

After all that Sarah had been through in pursuit of treatment for her depression, she came to the author in a state of acute demoralization. Have you ever been in a situation where you were completely demoralized, without hope of ever finding an answer? What did you do? If you have not been in such a situation, what do you think you would do to get out of such a state?

What is the basis of such complete demoralization?

Sarah's love of the piano was at times her salvation. Have you had something you loved like that? Where did you come by that gift? How has it helped you through hard times?

Is depression, as some would maintain, a choice?

Chapter 9 - Movement Three: Mozart's Student

Carol speaks of the legacy of her mother's influence in mixed terms. On the one hand, her mother instilled a passion for excellence. On the other, she weighted Carol down with expectations. Do you see your parents as a good influence or a bad influence, or like Carol's, in mixed terms. If you see them in mixed terms, how do you reconcile that discrepancy? If they are all good or all bad in your view, are you really being realistic? Is there something to be gained by seeking out the contributions, good or bad, at which you are less inclined to look?

Edmund Burke said: "All that is necessary for evil to triumph is that good men (and women) do nothing." Was Carol's pattern of taking up for the underdog (i.e. the exploited patient, the children depicted in the child porn) out of balance or was she actually a person trying to live in a way consistent with her values?

Do we tend to accept too much in the interest of "getting along?" Should we make a stand more often? In what area of your life might you be turning a blind eye to injustice or wrong?

How big a part do you think Carol's homosexuality played in her life and struggles? Why is homosexuality seemingly such a tough issue to deal with in a person's life?

It is often said in the clinical literature that in working with people who are gay and lesbian, you must always address the client's own homophobia. What does this mean? Do you agree? Why or why not?

Do you think the author crossed a line when he so plainly stated his personal theological opinion about homosexuality to Carol? Why or why not?

Do you think a therapist who believes homosexuality is either morally wrong or pathological can effectively treat a gay client?

Describe the perfect parents.

Epilogue

What do you think the author means when he says "Life always finds a way." Really? Always? Do you agree? If not, what are the limits? Are there times when life is ultimately meaningless? If so, what is our best response in those times?

The author ends with another reference to moments of Kairos. Do you think those moments are random, or can we do things that elicit Kairos experiences? Like what?

Even more ambitious, do you think one can make Kairos a discipline, to more or less live from that perspective?

The author refers to having "much to do" before the quiet comes. What are your most important priorities for you to accomplish in your time?

BIO

DR. DAVID SABINE is a psychologist in private practice in Wichita Falls, Texas. After a brief career in Christian urban ministry, he completed the Doctor of Philosophy in Clinical Psychology from the University of Louisville and a pre-doctoral fellowship at Yale University. He has four children. David is an avid sailor and when he is not writing or doing psychotherapy, he can often be found on a lake or the ocean at the helm of a sailboat.

Join the conversation personally on Facebook, Twitter, and Dr. Sabine's blog.
Get busy uncovering those moments of Kairos in your own life!

Website:
www.docsabine.com

Twitter:
http://www.twitter.com/docsabine

Facebook:
www.Facebook.com (Doc Sabine)